KRISHNA MOHAN AVANCHA

SECRETS OF PERSONAL BBRANDING UNVEILED

A practical guide

Contents

1

Introduction

At the point when social separating measures were set up, the Internet was the solitary association with the rest of the world for a large number of us. Web-based media stages, specifically, turned into the go-to sources for those of us searching for shopping options, news, and causes to help. This has underlined the significance of our web-based media profiles now like never before, particularly for those in positions of authority.

Building up an individual brand is indispensable now as individuals will keep on utilizing the Internet to sort out occasions, work, shop, lead gatherings, and even select individuals distantly even after the pandemic. This implies it is more probable individuals will find out about you online before they meet you face to face.

Selection representatives, expected customers, and even new companions frequently resort to web indexes to get familiar with you and what you do. A 2017 overview by worldwide counseling firm Harris Poll found that 70% of bosses utilize web-based media to screen up-and-comers prior to recruiting them. What you put out there, the qualities you offer, and how you impart these qualities, comprise your own image, and how individuals, particularly your clients, see you.

In the event that you are an entrepreneur, odds are your clients will look for you on the web, and view your pages via online media. Some of my companions feel it essential to become acquainted with the individual or individuals behind the brands and to see whether that individual's qualities are in a state of harmony with theirs, particularly during seasons of emergency. It is safe to say that they are rewarding the network? How are they supporting noble motivations?

Here are some central issues to remember when constructing your own image:

Characterize your crowd

Before you assemble your own image, figure out who your intended interest group is. Is it true that they are your business' customers? Is it true that they are selection representatives? Or on the other hand, would they say they are your section perusers? The sooner you sort this out, the simpler it will be for you to make the story you need to share, and one that they would identify with. On the off chance that you are a promoting master, at that point your crowd may incorporate entrepreneurs, showcasing fans, advertising understudies, and even writers. Along these lines, your story may incorporate effective showcasing efforts, gauging industry drifts, and in any event, advertising tips to entrepreneurs.

Manner of speaking

While speaking to your image, consider the value(s) you need to convey and the tone that reverberates best with your crowd. Is your tone easygoing? Is it instructive? What are your qualities?

One of the qualities that American news investor Oprah Winfrey embraces is to urge individuals to carry on with their best life, and that worth is conveyed through her messages, talks, and books.

When assembling your own image, show a big motivator for you and ensure that is handed-off through your tone and articulations. This reduces to your selection of words, and the kind of substance you share, re-tweet, or post on your Instagram page.

Thus, for instance, in the event that you need to urge individuals to accomplish their fantasies, at that point your page may incorporate examples of overcoming adversity of individuals who have moved all chances to accomplish their fantasies. You may share persuasive recordings, or even compose inspiring articles. Your message gradually turns into your brand name, and one that is simple for your clients to recognize as yours.

Individual portfolio

In the event that you are a planner, author, thought pioneer, or a promoting tactician, at that point it's basic to have an individual computerized portfolio or site that can feature your work. This permits expected customers and scouts to become familiar with your work. In the event that you will likely propel your profession and join associations, at that point LinkedIn is one online stage selection representative who will look into your encounters.

Your own image isn't just what you put via web-based media, yet how you hold yourself disconnected. In the event that you are an entrepreneur, you will be related to your image, and your standing is that of the brands. Much the same as building a brand, individual marking requires persistence and consistency. Remembering these components, notwithstanding, will facilitate the cycle.

2

Advantages of getting your personal brand

L et's be honest, no one gets up toward the beginning of the day thinking, "Gee, I need an individual brand today!"

The vast majority's emotions are more along the lines of, "For what reason should I trouble putting resources into my own image, without a doubt people know from my CV/LinkedIn profile why I'm acceptable!"

I have this discussion consistently with individuals who are so used to being important for a corporate marking machine – where honestly we mix away from plain sight and observe a bunch of brand rules.

Try not to misunderstand me, this can be fairly protected and satisfying... I should know. I worked with some astounding brands in my corporate days, including the Financial Times (think pink, smart and loads of pink champagne), The Institute of Directors (think suits, a rich history and world-driving chief preparing) and the Association of Colleges (think further schooling, subsidizing cuts and versatile and motivational school staff).

I was an aspiring advertiser (I actually am!) and saw supporting my organization's image as an aspect of my responsibilities depiction. I savored being essential for their image and fitting in – however much that you can actually

4

fit in when you're tall, light and German (think more straightforward than any other person in the room!)

Four years back everything changed for me. I took deliberate excess and was out of nowhere 'out there' without a 30-page brand book to follow, to reveal to me how to sound, what was OK to remark on and what to look like (OK, I'm misrepresenting a touch now!)

Thinking back, it was just when I began putting resources into my own image that things began to occur for me and my business Lollipop Social.

Thus, in case you're as yet in uncertainty, read on as I share what I accept are the critical advantages to building up your own image.

Makes you burrow profound and characterize your 'why'

One of the initial phases in building up an individual brand is characterizing your qualities and a big motivator for you. You need to wind up with an individual brand which is really you and which offers to your crowd.

Your 'why' is what is most important to you – what gets you up. Since let's be honest, making and maintaining your own business is no stroll in the recreation center. There are numerous highs and lows associated with working out of your customary range of familiarity consistently.

Knowing why you do what you do – and helping yourself to remember it – causes you manage these pinnacles and box.

It's truly enabling and empowering to distinguish your why and to utilize it as a feature of your story.

Causes you become acquainted with your crowd and how to identify with them

Individual marking should never be possible in seclusion.

Actually you're putting resources into it to develop your business, to get more cash-flow. Your marking needs to reverberate with the sort of individuals you need to work with.

An amazing individual brand is as much about your crowd for what it's worth about you. Ask yourself who your crowd are. What are their expectations, dreams and mentalities?

What are they keen on and how might you position yourself as an answer for the difficulties they face?

This understanding will assist you with making content that furnishes them with genuine worth, pulling in them characteristically to you and your image.

Go similarly as making your own image for the one individual you need to work with. Ponder what you appreciate. What would you be able to get paid well for? Where would you be able to discover the requirement for what you're advertising?

Makes selling 'you' simpler

In the event that you can't pitch yourself unquestionably, who will put stock in you and part with their money to work with you?

Presently, I view myself as an embraced Brit having lived here since 1995, and the facts demonstrate that we don't care for discussing why we're superior to every other person.

However, the significant thing to recollect is that an individual brand charac-terizes why we are unique in relation to every other person, and this will truly help you feel more certain about selling your administrations.

Numerous business visionaries battle with fraud disorder, which drives them to undercharge for their administrations. Building up your own image will support your pipeline and your capacity to sell more – and above all – at the correct cost!

Fabricates associations with the individuals you appreciate working with

Individuals purchase from individuals. How might you interface with the correct individuals in the event that you mix away from plain sight on social or are too corporate in your correspondences?

It's regular to feel anxious about sharing your weak side and defects, yet actually individuals are attracted to relatable individuals – and to their blemishes.

At the point when I was more youthful, I buckled down on relaxing my German inflection and rather direct way of passing on my messages. Presently, I incline toward my defects and play on them. So imagine a scenario in which I can't articulate words beginning with a 'v' or 'w' great. It makes me extraordinary! As a feature of my own image I utilize the odd German word and my Eastern German childhood as a component of my narrating.

Since I don't profess to be somebody else, individuals trust me. At the point when you watch one of my recordings, you'll see me similarly as I am the point at which you meet me face to face.

To me that is important. Also, it constructs deals. I probably won't engage individuals who pay attention to themselves as well, however that is fine since I like to have a great time when I'm working with customers.

Speaking the truth about what your identity is causes you pull in your clan – it's a mutually advantageous arrangement!

Makes you more paramount to your crowd

There are once in a while any pristine and weighty ideas. We as a whole have a comparative message, however you as the courier – you're genuinely exceptional.

An individual brand will assist you with releasing your innovativeness as a courier and help you own that message.

The present commercial center is overly occupied. For instance, on the off chance that you Google 'promoting advisor in Cambridge', you'll find more than 20 million outcomes.

This is much more motivation not to mix in and be vanilla. You must give the ideal individuals each motivation to like and recollect you, and individual marking is your easy route to this.

An important individual brand improves the probability of references from individual business visionaries as they recall you as well.

I hadn't acknowledged the amount of my business would come from references from individual business visionaries. It's a particularly extraordinary procurement channel and on the off chance that you don't sustain your own image, you will never tap in its latent capacity.

"At the point when I consider web-based media specialists (I know a few), your image is the one that stands apart the most. That implies you'll normally stick out in the event that somebody approaches me for a suggestion. This is the quintessence of why it's critical to assemble an individual brand: you improve opportunity to turn into somebody's top pick".

John Espirian, specialized publicist

Permits you to show your character

An all around characterized individual brand pushes your character to the bleeding edge – the most invigorating and viable approach to pass on your message.

For instance, in case you're enthusiastic about sympathy this will radiate through and draw in individuals who lean toward a steady methodology.

An extraordinary illustration of this is Lyndsay Cambridge and Youpreneur part Martin Huntbach who as of late dispatched their online enrollment Make Your Mark Online. During free site surveys in their Facebook gathering, their comprehension of how individuals can feel humiliated about their own site goes over right away. Both Lyndsay and Martin have legitimate individual brands which reverberate with their objective market.

Accept Andrew and Pete as another model. Their engaging and 'unboring' take on instructing individuals about substance showcasing pulls in the individuals who incline toward a funny bone when learning new things and feel attracted to them.

Your manner of speaking is your character on paper in advanced interchanges, so ensure it's pressed with character. Very frequently I see individuals turn too formal on LinkedIn, on their About Page and on their sites.

All things being equal, intensify your informing with your character to try not to mix away from plain sight. Standing apart is something to be thankful for!

Makes you and your business more relatable and constructs trust

A logo alone doesn't fabricate trust. Becoming more acquainted with the individual who is offering the administration does.

I was as of late met by Youpreneur part Alex Curtis, for his Lead Generation for Financial Services Podcast and we presumed that with regards to confiding in somebody with our life's reserve funds, trust is instrumental to the purchasing choice, similar to it is with numerous different buys.

In what manner will you assemble trust? A solid online presence? Indeed. Consistency? Indeed. However, showing yourself, giving your crowd a window into your reality with a predictable individual brand constructs trust over the long run. So when that individual has a requirement for the sort of administration you offer, not exclusively will you be top of psyche, yet you'll additionally have their trust.

Individuals just don't need flawlessness, they need relatable

Lift your effect via web-based media and ensure everything is predictable: the visual methodology, manner of speaking, content.

At the point when I began to situate myself as a showcasing specialist from London, I simply needed to shroud away and I was hesitant to be judged.

On a new webcast meet with Lee Jackson I truly opened up about this. My unique site had a green and purple PC on it – I just would not like to stick out.

Not a practical methodology when you need to assemble your image and a crowd of people. So I confronted my feelings of trepidation (actually do) and I put resources into myself. Gatherings, courses, instructing and a great deal of brand improvement.

My substance about the battles I confronted and how you can conquer them resounded with individuals which gave me more fortitude to share my story and to share promoting and individual marking tips for online media in my own remarkable manner. For instance my video blog is called WUNDERBAR The Marketing Efficiency Show.

Also, since I did my marking schoolwork and put resources into my visuals and substance advertising, stunning things have occurred.

My fantasy about relaunching my talking vocation in the wake of turning into a mum has become a reality

My substance draws in my intended interest group: site traffic developed by 300% longer than a year and online media references expanded by 270% longer than a year

Over the course of about 3 years, my profile via web-based media has detonated and I have cherished each moment of it.

I'll be dispatching my own instructing program Wunderstars this spring to help individuals face their web-based media fears and improve results on the web, FAST

Be patient and the difficult work will pay off.

3

Personal Brand for Job

The way to your fantasy profession is infrequently a straight way. Your objectives develop over the long haul, and it's characteristic to need to extend an alternate way or graph another course. Notwithstanding the purpose behind making a turn, there are a couple of things you ought to do prior to jumping into a pursuit of employment, including preparing your resume and making an individual site.

Another urgent apparatus: your own image. Your own image characterizes what your identity is and decides how others (counting future managers) will see you. While seeking after a lifelong change, it's particularly critical to develop your informing, repackage your experience, and show how your present aptitudes can be applied across various businesses.

I realize it's conceivable to take a vocation an alternate way without beginning without any preparation since I did exactly that. The way in to that achievement? Adjusting my own image to advance with my objectives, and utilizing my site to spread the message.

This is what you need to do. We additionally made a worksheet to help you through the cycle, which you can download here.

1. Perceive Positive Building Blocks

Your own image incorporates attributes and aptitudes that you've developed all through your vocation—and the initial step is to recognize which of those will mean the kinds of new jobs you're seeking after. (What's more, a significant number of them probably will!)

Suppose that you've filled in as a clerical specialist for a very long time. Your administrator work requires persistence, tender loving care, and a profound comprehension of the internal functions of an association that the vast majority never will see. Claiming those central qualities will help you make a vocation change in case you're attempting to take that jump.

As an innovative expert working in tech and account, I created substance and duplicate for huge loads of large brands. I cherished my work, yet I generally needed to expound on movement for magazines. Despite the fact that I didn't have any bylines in the field, I knew a huge load of the aptitudes from my corporate work moved to travel composing. All things considered, I went through my days exploring, composing, and hitting cutoff times. The control and relationship–building aptitudes at the core of my own image set the structure for working together with editors, as well.

Thing to do

At the point when you choose to grow or change your profession, consider how the structure squares of your own image mean your new objectives. Make a rundown of the attributes that will work well for you in your extended profession.

2. Diagram Your Path Forward

Much the same as how you utilize a guide (or how about we be genuine, GPS) to arrive at an objective, you need an arrangement to help develop your own image. A major piece of that advancement focuses on how you portray yourself and your work, at the end of the day, you need to accomplish the work to realize your fantasy vocation. Start by pinpointing your objective and laying out the experience you need to arrive.

At the point when I resolved to travel composing, I realized I needed to add different measurements to my range of abilities that represented I could accomplish the work. I put resources into an online photography class, a movement composing course, and an independent instructional exercise on pitching distributions. I contacted individuals I respect in the field for their information, read widely, and finished a couple of unpaid tasks before I began messaging editors. With the clearness that I could accomplish the work—and an extended portfolio displayed on my own site to demonstrate it—my fantasy tasks were nearer than at any other time.

Thing to do

Think about your optimal chance. What steps do you need to take to add another measurement to your own image? Envision each progression gathering speed to help you meet your objective. In case you don't know what steps you need to take, contact individuals in the business for their point of view on the best way to get from a to z.

3. Advance Your Messaging

Whenever you've considered your basic qualities and outlined the means to extend your vocation, you're prepared to advance the informing around your own image. Now, it merits putting resources into or refreshing an individual site through a simple to utilize web designer like Squarespace. I love that it's very reasonable, has a natural simplified interface, and gives many formats to browse—causing you fabricate an expert site that catches your character and story.

Ask a companion who is acceptable with a camera—or an expert—to take a few photos of you for the site. Next, you'll need to consider how you need to change your presentation, professional training, and mastery to catch the new brand you're wanting to make. You don't need to invalidate all that you've done previously; all things considered, expand on the establishment that you've just settled.

Here's a when that shows how I developed my own image to assist me with landing positions as a movement author:

Previously: I team up with brands and distributions to recount stories that engage advanced perusers. Through elevated level informing, wise articles, and clear copywriting, I set up the correct tone, voice, and reason to situate my customers as industry pioneers.

After: I team up with brands and distributions to recount stories that engage computerized perusers. Through significant level informing, astute articles, and clear copywriting, I set up the correct tone, voice, and reason to hoist my customers' according to their crowd. On the ends of the week, I additionally fill in as a contributing travel essayist and picture taker for distributions like Vogue, Mic, Travel + Leisure, Condé Nast Traveler, and The Week.

See what I did there? It's simpler than you might suspect to extend your own image to line up with new objectives. As your vocation advances, don't avoid pushing ahead, regardless of whether it seems like a danger.

Thing to do

Change your own image informing on your site and online media to reflect what you need to do pushing ahead. Play with the language and don't avoid possessing your qualities as an expert.

With regards to your own image, you're steering the ship. You can pick how to portray your qualities and the manner in which you need to develop. By expanding on your best attributes, graphing a make way, and tweaking your informing, you'll be well headed to the professional change you had always wanted.

4

Personal Brand for Business

1. You Are Synonymous With Your Brand

Conveying quality items and administrations are table stakes, yet in a jam-packed market, your own image is the differentiator. Position yourself as a confided in master in your field through substance, talking commitment, and different vehicles. Indeed (and particularly) in a commoditized business, your own image encourages you to stand apart from clients.

2. You'll Attract The Right Customers

An unmistakable and solid individual brand helps possible clients or customers know you're not the one for them. This is extraordinary information for developing your business for several distinct reasons. You won't invest energy attempting to offer to individuals who probably wouldn't accepting from you in any case. You'll likewise give your optimal customers significantly more motivation to associate with you and become faithful clients.

3. It Can Work In Conjunction With Your Customer Service Efforts

While your own image is undeniably significant, zeroing in on the picture of your business to abundance can neutralize you when it brings about time away from planning how best to serve your clients. Appear from a position of the administration. The most ideal approach to exhibit what working with you implies is to comprehend your customers and assist them with taking care of the difficult issues that keep them up around evening time.

4. Clients Buy Emotions, Not Products

Clients consistently look for passionate trust first prior to purchasing anything. You can at present know a great deal or offer the best items, yet on the off chance that you don't pass on your incentive inwardly, you will fizzle. Individual marking just as organization marking is consistently about genuineness, trust, and positive feelings. Really at that time wraps up of the incentive come.

5. You Can Develop And Demonstrate Your Value

There are numerous ways we can create and exhibit our mastery and incentive as we try to fabricate and fortify our own image. Search for occasions to be a visitor master on industry online classes and webcasts, compose industry-centered articles, be a visitor speaker at a college, and so forth As you begin to pick up this experience, the open doors will snowball and you can share your worth!

6. Individuals Buy You What Your Brand Stands For

At the point when you are a startup or an independent venture, possibilities and clients are getting "you." You need to have a solid individual brand. Something else, in what capacity will individuals realize you exist? At the point when individuals purchase from you and become clients, they are purchasing what your image depends on, which is your guarantee to them. At the point when clients become steadfast, raving fans, that reinforces your own image and develops your business.

7. You'll Build Credibility And Trust

Early introductions purchase an entrance to business achievement. Solid individual brands loan believability and mastery to that early introduction. Future accomplices or clients search for confiding seeing someone, information, and responsibility. Decisions are made rapidly and individual brands just get us up until now. We should quickly convey with demonstrable skill, results, and follow up. There is nobody single projectile.

8. You Can Speak Directly To Your Customer With Great Content

I have consistently incorporated an individual brand-building perspective with our vocation and outplacement administrations. There might be a ton of substance and things being distributed out there, however, there are not a lot of valuable pieces. Follow the pattern with an author or a supervisor. Leave this essayist alone your guide and begin distributing articles that issue, are elegantly composed, and address your objective market crowd.

9. It Encourages Clients To Recommend You

A solid individual brand reinforces the validity of a business. In the event that you need to turn into a perceived name that individuals trust, you need to try to do what you say others should do, make web-based media perceivability, and gain authority through organizations or systems administration. Consistently, ask yourself, "How might I conclude a commitment with a possibility or a customer so they will prescribe me to other people?" Experiment with your thoughts.

10. You'll Forge Real Connections

Understanding the significance of social and passionate associations with focused customers is key for brand value. The degree of profitability is acknowledged when shoppers can undoubtedly get to and perceive an item or administration, feel genuinely associated, buy, and socially draw in with it. At the point when clients become diplomats of the brand, force is assembled and positive outcomes are figured out.

11. Your Brand Stands For Your Character, Culture, And Principles

Regardless of whether it's your organization image or your own image, your image represents the character, the way of life, and the rules that you operationalize every single day. One approach to keep on fortifying your image is to not change or waiver from your standards, your guarantees, and your responsibility towards showing the nature of greatness you convey.

12. It Communicates How You Show Up To The World

Your image imparts how you appear in the world. It's a mix of your motivation, your qualities, your qualities, and your uniqueness. By living and displaying your image, you set up validity and trust, which is key for building and supporting connections and is the center of your business. The way to stretching out your own image is to stay devoted to your image in any event, when it might change.

13. It Is The Essence Of Your Business

Your image is the substance of your business; it's a particular and suffering angle that resounds with the customer. Ensure all items and administrations related with your business tie back to this brand pith and make certain to secure it. Entrepreneurs can take their own image to the following level by assessing brand angles quarterly and refreshing in like manner i.e., site, composing, showcasing, and so forth

5

Determine & Prioritize Your Values and Passions

With regards to carrying on with an all-around planned life, guarantee that you know what your identity is and what you need.

Living purposefully includes more than just thinking about certain objectives and attempting to contact them. It's tied in with venturing somewhat more profound into what your identity is, the thing that makes you wake up, what you appreciate doing, and what you're acceptable at!

Understanding your center—your qualities, your interests, and your qualities—will assist you with making a life that is characterized by goal and will empower you to set objectives that are genuinely lined up with what your identity is and what you deeply desire.

Consider the big picture for a second. What is the main thing about a business? Obviously, it's their basic beliefs. A decent entrepreneur will invest a ton of energy characterizing their basic beliefs. The explanation? It is a strong establishment in which the business can develop. The equivalent is valid for your own life also. In case we're not in contact with our center—our qualities, interests, and qualities—at that point we'll struggle living purposefully.

In the weeks ahead, we will investigate more about carrying on with an all-around planned life and taking a gander at how precisely that separates basically. Today, we should reveal what you can do to burrow profound and find precisely what your qualities, interests, and qualities are—building the establishment to adjust your objectives, plans, and activities with your center this year!

Prepared to begin? How about we start by investigating every one of these components top to bottom at this point!

Qualities

First up, how about we investigate values. These are things that issue more to you than anything on earth. Possibly it's your family, or maybe there are causes that you care colossally about. While there are various records accessible online that you can use to single out from to recognize your basic beliefs, ensure you invest some energy looking through profound and considering yourself. Would it be that YOU care about? Probably there are a large number of things that you can consider! Record them all.

On the off chance that you are battling to think of a rundown, here are a couple of inquiries you could pose to yourself:

- What drives you?

- What are you enthusiastic about?

· How might individuals around you depict you?

· Consider important minutes: for what reason would they say they were so significant?

· Consider baffling minutes: for what reason would they say they were disappointing?

· What must you have in your life besides the rudiments?

Whatever it is that makes it to your rundown, this will give you clearness on what is generally critical to you. This will permit you to guarantee that you're building connections and settling on professional decisions that will empower you and keep you inspired.

Interests

Your interests are regions where you'd love to concentrate, regardless of whether you're not getting paid for it! What kinds of causes and thoughts set your brain ablaze? What aspects of your life might you want to dedicate more opportunity to? These are regions that you'll be the most inventive, and most in your component.

Consider the possibility that you don't know where your interests lie. Consider asking yourself the accompanying inquiries to get your brain thinking the correct way:

- What are you inquisitive about?

- What fulfills your heart?

- Where do your inclinations lie?

- What might you do if cash wasn't an item?

- Where might you invest your energy in the event that you had more hours in the day?

Being disengaged from your interests implies that you'll be unfulfilled or separated from your work or even life all in all. In any case, by setting aside the effort to distinguish what drives you, you can pick up clearness on aspects of your life that may have to change, or steps that you need to take to expand your satisfaction.

Qualities

What are you acceptable at? Frequently, the things that we're extraordinary at, are additionally those things that present to us the most euphoria and satisfaction. You feel anxious to play out these assignments—upbeat, willing, and spurred.

Todd Kashdan, a brain research educator at George Mason University, says that "You can see somebody feels invigorated and roused when they're utilizing a center strength." What makes YOU wake up?

Not certain where your center qualities lie? Think about doing some perception! What things have companions, family, associates, or even total outsiders commended you on? What comes effectively to you? What do you do interestingly well? These are your qualities! Your own mix of these abilities is extraordinarily yours. Having obviously recognized qualities can assist you with building a vocation or permit you to distinguish which zones you'll need to zero in on when developing your aptitudes, chipping in, or helping other people.

These components cooperate to speak to an alternate feature of your character! At the point when assembled, they contain your center! These will assist you in finding your optimal profession, fortify your connections, and discover pursuits that will leave you feeling the most satisfied.

It is safe to say that you are prepared to begin finding your center? Make certain to get your FREE Core Elements Worksheet. At that point, will work on finding your own qualities, centers, and qualities.

What's more, make certain to tune in one week from now—to become familiar with driving an all-around planned life.

6

Define Your Key Traits

What makes somebody what their identity is? Every individual has a thought character type — on the off chance that they are bubbly or held, touchy or tough. Analysts who attempt to coax out the study of what our identity is characterized character as individual contrasts in the manner individuals will in general think, feel, and carry on.

There are numerous approaches to quantify character; however, analysts have generally abandoned attempting to isolate humanity conveniently into types. All things considered, they center around character characteristics.

The most broadly acknowledged of these characteristics are the Big Five:

Transparency

Uprightness

Extraversion

Appropriateness

Neuroticism

Advantageously, you can recall these characteristics with the convenient OCEAN memory helper (or, on the off chance that you like, CANOE works, as well).

The Big Five were created during the 1970s by two examination groups. These groups were driven by Paul Costa and Robert R. McCrae of the National Institutes of Health and Warren Norman and Lewis Goldberg of the University of Michigan at Ann Arbor and the University of Oregon, as indicated by Scientific American.

The Big Five are the fixings that make up every individual's character. An individual may have a scramble of transparency, a ton of principles, a normal measure of extraversion, a lot of pleasantness, and basically no neuroticism by any means. Or on the other hand, somebody could be unpalatable, hypochondriac, withdrawn, scrupulous, and scarcely open by any means. This is what every characteristic involves:

Receptiveness

Transparency is shorthand for "receptiveness to encounter." People who are high in receptiveness appreciate the experience. They're interested and acknowledge workmanship, creative mind, and new things. The proverb of the open individual may the same old thing all the time wears out a person's soul."

Individuals low in receptiveness are the polar opposite: They want to adhere to their propensities, keep away from new encounters, and presumably aren't the bravest eaters. Changing character is typically viewed as an extreme cycle, yet receptiveness is a character characteristic that has been demonstrated to be liable to change in adulthood. In a recent report, individuals who took psilocybin, or psychedelic "wizardry mushrooms," turned out to be more open after the experience. The impact endured in any event a year, recommending that it very well may be lasting.

Talking about test drug use, California's take a stab at anything society is no legend. An investigation of character characteristics across the United States delivered in 2013 found that transparency is generally common on the West Coast.

Uprightness

Individuals who are honest are coordinated and have a solid feeling of obligation. They're trustworthy, trained, and accomplishment centered. You won't discover upright sorts streaming off on round-the-world excursions with just a knapsack; they're organizers.

Individuals low in scruples are more unconstrained and freewheeling. They may incline toward thoughtlessness. The principle is a useful attribute to have, as it has been connected to accomplishment in school and at work.

Extraversion

Extraversion versus contemplation is potentially the most conspicuous character quality of the Big Five. The greater amount of an extravert somebody is, the even more an extrovert they are. Extraverts are garrulous, friendly, and draw energy from swarms. They will in general be self-assured and bright in their social communications.

Thoughtful people, then again, need a lot of alone time, maybe in light of the fact that their minds cycle social cooperation in an unexpected way. Introspection is regularly mistaken for bashfulness, yet the two aren't the equivalent. Timidity infers a dread of social communications or powerlessness to work socially. Loners can be entirely enchanting at parties — they simply incline toward solo or little gathering exercises.

Suitability

Suitability quantifies the degree of an individual's glow and benevolence. The more pleasant somebody is, the almost certain they are to be trusted, useful, and caring. Unpleasant individuals are cold and dubious of others, and they're more averse to collaborate.

Men who are high in pleasantness are decided to be better artists by ladies, recommending that body development can flag character. (Uprightness likewise makes for good artists, as indicated by a similar 2011 examination.) But in the work environment, unsavory men really procure more than pleasing folks. Unpleasant ladies didn't show a similar compensation advantage, proposing that a straightforward disposition is interestingly gainful to men.

Being jealous, which can prompt individuals to be seen as not pleasant, was discovered to be the most well-known character type out of the four examinations by a report distributed in August 2016 in the diary Science Advances. Jealous individuals feel undermined when another person is more fruitful than they are.

Neuroticism

To get neuroticism, look no farther than George Costanza of the long-running sitcom "Seinfeld." George is celebrated for his anxieties, which show faults in his broken guardians. He stresses over everything, fixates on germs and illness, and once leaves a place of employment since his nervousness over not approaching a private restroom is excessively overpowering.

George might be high on the neuroticism scale, however, the character quality is genuine. Individuals high in neuroticism stress much of the time and effectively slip into nervousness and misery. In the event that everything is working out positively, masochist individuals will in general discover things to stress over. One 2012 investigation found that when masochist individuals with great compensations procured raises, the additional pay really made them less upbeat.

Conversely, individuals who are low in neuroticism will in general be sincerely steady and balanced.

Commercial

Obviously, neuroticism is connected with a lot of awful wellbeing results. Psychotic individuals kick the bucket more youthful than the genuinely steady, conceivably in light of the fact that they go to tobacco and liquor to facilitate their nerves.

Potentially the creepiest reality about neuroticism, however, is that parasites can cause you to feel that way. What's more, we're not discussing the characteristic uneasiness that may accompany realizing that a tapeworm has made a home in your gut. Undetected disease by the parasite Toxoplasma gondii may make individuals more inclined to neuroticism, a recent report found.

Detecting and instinct allude to how individuals want to assemble data about the world, regardless of whether through solid data (detecting) or passionate sentiments (instinct). Thinking and feeling allude to how individuals decide. Thinking types go with rationale while feeling types follow their hearts.

The Myers-Briggs framework is balanced with the judging/discernment division, which depicts how individuals decide to interface with the world. Passing judgment on sorts like conclusive activity, while seeing sorts lean toward open alternatives. The framework further distinguishes 16 character types dependent on a mix of four of the classes, prompting depictions, for example, ISTP, ENFP, ESFJ, and so forth

The utilization of the Myers-Briggs is dubious, as examination proposes that types don't relate well with work fulfillment or capacities.

Would personality be able to change?

Perhaps. An examination distributed in the January 2017 diary Psychological Bulletin integrated 207 distributed exploration papers and found that character might be changed through treatment. "For the individuals who need to change their life partner tomorrow, which many individuals need to do, I don't hold out a lot of trust in them," said study scientist Brent Roberts, a social and character therapist at the University of Illinois. Notwithstanding, he proceeded, "in case you're willing to zero in on one part of yourself, and you're willing to go at it deliberately, there's presently expanded idealism that you can influence change in that space."

7

Develop Your Personal Image

What is mental self-view?

The mental self-portrait is the individual view, or mental picture, that we have of ourselves. The mental self-portrait is an "inside word reference" that depicts the qualities of oneself, including such things as savvy, excellent, revolting, skilled, egotistical, and kind. These attributes structure and aggregate portrayal of our resources (qualities) and liabilities (shortcomings) as we see them.

How is mental self-view created?

Mental self-view as a result of learning. Youth impacts, for example, guardians and parental figures, affect our mental self-view. They are mirrors reflecting back to us a picture of ourselves. Our encounters with others, for example, educators, companions, and family add to the picture in the mirror. Connections fortify our opinion and feel about ourselves.

The picture we find in the mirror might be a genuine or mutilated perspective on who we truly are. In light of this view, we grow either a positive or a negative mental self-view. The qualities and shortcomings we have received an influence on how we act today. We persistently learn and assess ourselves in a few zones, for example, actual appearance (How would I look?), execution (How am I doing?), and connections (How significant am I?).

With a positive mental self-view, we perceive and own our resources and possibilities while being sensible about our liabilities and impediments. With a negative mental self-portrait, we center around our deficiencies and shortcomings, twisting disappointment and blemishes.

Mental self-view is significant on the grounds that how we consider ourselves influences how we feel about ourselves and how we collaborate with others and our general surroundings. A positive mental self-portrait can help our physical, mental, social, enthusiastic, and profound prosperity. Then again, a negative mental self-portrait can diminish our fulfillment and capacity to work in these regions.

How might we make a positive mental self-portrait?

The mental self-portrait isn't for all time fixed. Some portion of our mental self-view is dynamic and evolving. We can figure out how to build up a more advantageous and more precise perspective on ourselves, accordingly testing the contortions in the mirror. Mental self-portrait change happens over a long period. A sound mental self-portrait begins with figuring out how to acknowledge and adore ourselves. It additionally implies being acknowledged and adored by others.

- Explicit strides to build up a positive mental self-view
- Take a mental self-portrait stock.
- Make a rundown of your positive characteristics.
- Request that huge others depict your positive characteristics.
- Characterize individual objectives and destinations that are sensible and quantifiable.
- Defy thinking twists.
- Recognize and investigate the effect of youth marks.

- Abstain from contrasting yourself with others.
- Build up your qualities.
- Figure out how to adore yourself.
- Give positive assertions.
- Recollect that you are one of a kind.
- Recollect how far you have come.
- What is self-perception?

Self-perception is essential for mental self-view. Our self-perception incorporates more than what we resemble or how others see us. It additionally alludes to how we think, feel, and respond to our own impression of our actual ascribes.

Self-perception improvement is influenced by social pictures and the impact of family, friends, and others. A positive self-perception adds to improved mental change (less discouragement, positive self-esteem, life fulfillment, less relational nervousness, less dietary issues). Bends in our intuition add to a negative self-perception.

How might we upgrade our self-perception?

Self-perception isn't fixed. Our body encounters change as we become more established, and each stage in our life is related to self-perception markers. Keeping a positive self-perception is a long-lasting cycle.

Changing negative self-perception implies more than changing our body. It implies changing how we think, feels, and respond to our bodies. Weight the board and medical procedure are two different ways to change the body. Figuring out how to have a positive relationship with a blemished body builds the capacity to get thinner. Medical procedures can be a method for changing how we see ourselves. Broad outside rebuilding, in any case, additionally requires broad inside changes in self-perception.

Explicit strides to upgrade self-perception:

- Investigate your own self-perception with its qualities and constraints.
- Face thinking contortions identified with your body.
- Challenge deluding suppositions about body appearance.
- Acknowledge and love what your identity is.
- Be alright with your body.
- Have positive encounters with your body.
- Be a companion to your body with positive insistences.

8

Define Your Target Audience

As an advertiser, understanding your intended interest group is fundamental. This data will characterize each advertising plan and procedure you execute. Circulating an advertisement during the Super Bowl may appear as though an extraordinary method to be seen by however many individuals as could be expected under the circumstances, yet it is likewise costly. Moreover, just a fourth of the watchers would really be keen on your item. Realizing that your intended interest group peruses a specific distribution or watches a specific show implies that your advertisement will be seen by fewer individuals, yet the opportune individuals. For instance, in the event that you sell running shoes, advertisements in running magazines might be a superior fit for your intended interest group. Choosing the privileged media is basic for accomplishing advertising ROI on your endeavors.

Notwithstanding expanding ROI, understanding your objective market permits you to assemble connections and better speak with buyers. You can create imaginative that addresses explicit personas, and create brands that correspond with the interests and estimations of those well on the way to buy the item. This is particularly significant at a time where consumers anticipate that each advertisement should be customized and profoundly focused on. Truth be told, 80% of purchasers state they are bound to work with a brand that offers customized collaborations.

What Are the Types of Target Audiences?

Target crowds can be portioned further into classes that reference, plan, area, interests, and then some. How about we investigate instances of ways that you can separate your intended interest group:

Interest

Separate gatherings out dependent on their different advantages, including pastimes and amusement inclinations. This can help you make information-driven, exceptionally customized informing that permits you to interface with your crowd in significant manners that can help drive brand dedication.

Buy Intention

Characterize gatherings of individuals who are searching for a particular item, for example, another theater setup or vehicle. This will assist you with understanding your crowd's problem areas so you can make customized informing that tends to their requirements.

Subcultures

Subcultures allude to gatherings of individuals who share a typical encounter, for example, music types or amusement fandoms. By seeing a portion of your intended interest group's inspirations, you can all the more likely comprehend who you're attempting to associate with.

The Difference Between Target Audience and Target Market

An objective market is the arrangement of customers that an organization intends to offer to or reach with showcasing exercises. An intended interest group is the gathering or section inside that target market that is being served notices. This makes the intended interest group a more explicit subset of an objective market.

To return to the running shoe model, your objective market is long-distance runners, yet state you are having an arrangement at your Boston area. The intended interest group for an advertisement advancing the deal would be forthcoming sprinters in the Boston Marathon, not all long-distance runners.

Target crowd can frequently be utilized reciprocally with the target market, as it is a particular subset of the biggest market gathering. In any case, the target market doesn't generally mean an objective crowd.

Understanding the Roles of Your Target Audience

A significant advance in understanding your intended interest group is to go past learning their segment data, and comprehend what job they play in the way to buy. These jobs can regularly be partitioned into the accompanying classes:

The Decision Maker: This is the individual who at last settles on the buy choice. Sometimes, the chief is equivalent to the ally, yet in different cases they are unique. At the point when unique, you should recognize this and stuff advertisements to the leader. Take, for instance, the change of the Old Spice brand in 2010. The brand needed to redo their item to interest a more youthful age. While investigating, the group found that while men may, at last, wear their item, ladies were making the buys, driving their imaginative group to zero in on this intended interest group.

The Supporter: The ally might not have the ability to settle on the choice, however, they will affect whether a thing gets purchased. For instance, a youngster may not straightforwardly make a buy, yet on the off chance that they need something for Christmas, they impact that choice. This is the reason it is essential to create information that addresses buyers in both of these jobs.

7 Ways to Determine Your Target Audience

To decide your intended interest group, you should invest energy investigating the information you get from customer commitment, assessing current purchasers and buy drifts, and enhancing as new data is uncovered.

The accompanying advances should assist you with understanding your intended interest group:

1. Examine Your Customer Base and Carry Out Client Interviews

Probably the most ideal approach to figure out who your intended interest group is to see who as of now purchases your item or administration. How old would they say they are, the place where do they live, what are their inclinations? A decent method to get familiar with this is through drawing in on social or circulating client reviews.

2. Lead Market Research and Identify Industry Trends

Take a gander at the statistical surveying for your industry to figure out where there are openings in assistance that your item can fill. Take a gander at patterns for comparative items to see where they are centering endeavors, at that point sharpen in further on your items one of a kind worth.

3. Dissect Competitors

Advertisers can gain proficiency with a ton by seeing contenders see what their identity is usually offering to, and how they go about it. It is safe to say that they are utilizing on the web or disconnected channels? It is safe to say that they are zeroing in on the leader or the ally?

4. Make Personas

Making personas is an extraordinary method to bore down into the particular sections that make up your objective audience. This is particularly useful in the event that you have an item that bids to a wide area of shoppers. Personas permit you to decide the overall socioeconomics, characters, and needs of your objective customers. The persona of "Fran First-Time Runner" will address unexpected requirements in comparison to "Sam Seasoned Pro." Personas are made dependent on information, overviews, advanced commitment and some other data advertisers can pull from to give a more complete perspective on the purchasers. This may incorporate most loved interests, network shows, distributions, and so forth It is suggested that advertisers create somewhere in the range of three and five personas.

5. Characterize Who Your Target Audience Isn't

There will unquestionably be shoppers who are near your objective segment, however, who won't follow up on informing. Attempt to be explicit in figuring out who your crowd is and who it isn't. Is your segment ladies, or ladies between the ages of 20 and 40? Realizing this will shield your groups from committing promotion dollars to fragments that won't yield returns.

6. Ceaselessly Revise

As you assemble more information and interface with clients, you will get an undeniably precise comprehension of your intended interest groups. In light of this data, you should continually advance and sharpen personas to accomplish the best outcomes.

7. Use Google Analytics

Google Analytics offers broad information about the clients visiting your site. This data can be utilized to decide key experiences, for example, what channels your intended interest group is coming from or what kind of substance they're drawing in and interfacing with the most, permitting you to settle on more information-driven choices during the media arranging measure.

Step by step instructions to Create Target Personas with The Right Demographics

We've just settled that making personas can be another incredible method to get crowds. Statistical surveying combined with customer meetings can give you better bits of knowledge into what your customers read, think, and worth. This offers significant comprehension into which sources your crowd uses and trusts. When fabricating these out, think about utilizing the accompanying socioeconomics and identifiers:

- Age
- Sex
- Area
- Pastimes
- Pay
- Instruction level
- Calling
- Conjugal status
- Who they trust
- What they read/observe

Furthermore, investigate the accompanying:

- Your present client base
- Who your rivals are focusing on
- Step by step instructions to Reach Your Target Audience

Whenever you've made personas, the subsequent stage is to discover media that objectives these particular sections. The following are a few apparatuses to kick you off:

Media Kits

Media packs from distributors give an away from of the crowd portions they reach. These can be separated by work titles, pay levels, or side interests relying upon the brand. While choosing where to contribute advertisement dollars, advertisers ought to guarantee that auxiliary crowds are excluded from these sums. For instance, magazines are regularly given to loved ones. This long time span of usability is useful for advertisers, yet ought not to be incorporated when choosing where to purchase as they are gauges. Utilize the paid endorsers when settling on choices or haggling on expense.

Nielsen Ratings

Utilizing measurable samplings, Nielsen can foresee the number of family units that see a specific show. Albeit early evening may appear to be an extraordinary wagered to contact wide crowds, you may find that more specialty shows in the early or late periphery will arrive at your intended interest group for a small amount of the expense. This is particularly evident as more stations and shows make TV profoundly divided.

Social

Web-based media permits you to target promotions dependent on different socioeconomics and interests. In spite of the fact that the crowd can be exact, various socioeconomics devours media in an unexpected way. A few clients may not be open to business-related advertisements on Instagram, however, may react all the more decidedly on Facebook. It is additionally critical to gauge the accomplishment of various sorts of promotions on these stages – like presentation versus local. Test different stages to perceive what drives results.

Outsider Information

Advertising investigation stages, for example, the Marketing Measurement and Attribution Platform can assist you in recognizing what sources your intended interest groups incessant or TV programs they watch. While choosing an accomplice, research how these organizations recognize how to arrive at the intended interest groups.

The most effective method to Reach your Audience at the Right Time

When advertising to the presently engaged shoppers, it isn't just about realizing where to contact them, yet in addition when to contact them. As buyers become more proficient at blocking informing out, promoting in the correct second will deliver profits.

There are a few significant contemplations to guarantee right-time promotion across different channels:

TV

With the creation of DVR, watchers at this point don't need to endure ads. This implies that even with the correct objective crowd, you can't really ensure sees on advertisements appeared in any show's break. While arranging TV spaces, center around either being the primary business before a break or the last one toward the finish of a break. Stunningly better is live TV (counting the late-night news or games). Since these are life, it's ensured that more individuals are viewing right now instead of squeezing the quick forward catch.

Radio

Since audience members frequently switch radio broadcasts at a business break, make a point to book promotions at either the start of the break or the end if conceivable. Additionally, make certain to focus on DMAs (Designated

Market Areas). DMAs are given by Nielsen and depend on sign strength. For instance, the Boston market likewise incorporates Rhode Island and Southern New Hampshire. It is imperative to remember this, in light of the fact that albeit radio is an incredible method to arrive at neighborhood shoppers, it might likewise incorporate audience members outside your objective district.

Email

When booking a blast with a source, think about its planning. Fridays are a typical day for individuals to take off, so sending an email out on an alternate day may build your open rates (except if the information says something else).

Burdens of Target Audiences

In spite of the fact that intended interest groups are an extraordinary apparatus, advertisers ought to recall that extra open doors may exist in the commercial center. In the event that groups need to reposition themselves, they may better associate with an alternate segment. There may likewise be use cases for items that haven't been thought of. Consolidating objective crowds with investigation apparatuses can help distinguish a portion of these botched chances to additionally exploit them.

9

Build Your Online Presence

At this point, you presumably realize that you need an online presence. You need an online space to help construct your business, sell items, or get your name out there.

The interesting part is sorting out some way to do it and computing the amount it will cost.

The most serious issue here is setting off course. Picking some unacceptable stage toward the start can cost you months in backtracking (also the financial expense of setting it up).

I've committed this error myself. I've set up sites on two, three distinct stages prior to acknowledging I might have gone through less cash and diminished the issue on the off chance that I'd quite recently done the exploration and picked the correct course in any case.

I'm by all account not the only one by the same token. At the point when I asked 27 specialists their greatest publishing content to a blog botches, a major small bunch said they lamented picking some unacceptable stage and neglected to outline the correct arrangement from the very first moment.

This is the guide I wish I had when I was beginning. A straightforward instructional exercise that causes you to sort out which is the best stage for you.

That is the key here. There is no ideal method to set up an online presence, just the correct one for your objectives and aspirations.

At a brisk look, here are the four we're taking a gander at:

A web-based media stage

Since not every person needs a site.

WordPress.org

A middle of the road progressed site building stage with unlimited authority.

Wix

A basic, fledgling web designer for portfolios and online journals.

Shopify

Basic web designer explicitly for online stores.

Second, we will sort out some way to develop your online presence. Lamentably, a site or web-based media page all alone won't mysteriously pull in guests. We'll acquaint you with a small bunch of ways you can effectively drive individuals to it and develop your online presence.

(Back To Top)

Which Platform Is Right For Your Online Presence?

1. A Social Media Page

Experts – It's free, basic, and low support.

Cons – Less power over plan and calculation changes.

Cost of arrangement – Completely free.

Find out more – Facebook/Instagram

A few organizations and people needn't bother with a site. It's an issue and cost that can be counter-beneficial.

Now and then, a Facebook page or Instagram account is the most ideal approach to construct a group of people, interface with individuals, and keep them refreshed. These are stages that your clients are now acquainted with and there are 1.6 billion dynamic clients hanging tight for you!

A bistro or eatery, for instance, could work with just a Facebook or Instagram profile. They could transfer new pictures, keep the menu refreshed, speak with clients, advance occasions, and feature uncommon offers all from one spot.

They could even utilize a Facebook module to take reservations. A site for this situation may very well convolute things and split the crowd. All things considered, center around building one incredible channel.

Concerning video content and contributing to a blog, Facebook cooks for this as well. Local recordings on Facebook presently hit 8 billion perspectives day by day, and their Instant Articles permit you to distribute online journals without a site.

Also, Facebook has a fantastic advert stage, so you can focus on a crowd of people and drive them directly to your page (more on Facebook adverts later).

The disadvantage of just having an online media page is that you're helpless before their choices. On the off chance that Facebook changes their calculation to restrict your span (which they do consistently), you may need to pay to associate with your devotees.

You're likewise restricted regarding the plan. You can transfer pictures and headers, yet the bounds of Facebook or Instagram's format might be disappointing for a few.

Above all, in the event that you need to sell something, Facebook isn't ideal. In spite of the fact that modules are accessible, Facebook consistently changes which modules it permits. Your shop could be taken out without notice.

2. WordPress Site

Professionals – Complete control and limitless potential.

Cons – Cost of support, specialized expertise required.

Cost of arrangement – Starts at $5-$20 every month for facilitating and area.

Find out more – WordPress facilitating

WordPress is the most ideal decision on the off chance that you need your own site with full oversight and adaptability. WordPress powers 25% of all sites out there, so it's a trusted, regarded stage.

You can do pretty much anything with WordPress. Fabricate an online store, make a portfolio site, post web journals and substance, construct an associate webpage. You can have adverts, gather email addresses, bring in cash, and maintain an online business all from one spot.

It's adaptable as well. It controls the absolute greatest destinations on the web, including The New Yorker, Techcrunch, Variety, Mashable, and Time Inc, however it works similarly also for an individual blog.

WordPress locales are adjustable, so you can customize your online presence with any plan or style you like. WordPress accompanies a large group of free layouts (or 'topics'). Each can be changed to your inclination, or an expert website specialist can make something totally interesting without any preparation for you. (Or then again in the event that you like a paid participation will concede you admittance to wonderful premium subjects.)

This control and adaptability do, nonetheless, includes some major disadvantages. Despite the fact that WordPress itself is free, the design that accompanies it isn't. You'll require a web have (this is basically a bit of web land your site sits on) and a space name, www.my-website.com.

Picking a decent web to have is as significant as the site itself. It adds to stack speed, security, and execution. Our host correlation table here is a decent spot to begin – The great (and sensibly valued) web facilitating.

Making and keeping a WordPress site additionally requires a component of specialized ability. WordPress guarantee you can set up and introduce inside 5 minutes, yet getting your site ready for action takes somewhat more than that.

There is an expectation to absorb information and it will burn through a lot of your time, particularly on the off chance that you need to change the plan, update it routinely, and improve execution.

On the off chance that you like the sound of having your own site, however, don't need such a great amount of problem, there is another choice, Wix.

3. Wix

Stars – Simple, simplified plan, simple arrangement.

Cons – Limited contrasted with WordPress.

Cost of arrangement – Free, yet it merits moving up to the superior designs for an individual area (beginning at $4.50).

Wix is like WordPress however without all the whine. Without a doubt, it's more restricted, however not every person needs a muddled rundown of highlights.

The excellence of Wix is its effortlessness. They deal with facilitating, stockpiling, execution, and all the specialized stuff in the background. You can simply sign in and add content.

All the formats are simplified, so you can spread out your site with no coding at all. The free formats are for the most part more classy than WordPress, which will engage specialists and innovative experts.

The Wix layouts loan themselves to basic portfolio locales and web journals and that is the place where it flourishes. Wix offers the mechanics for setting up an online store, however, WordPress or Shopify (coming up straightaway) offer a superior stage for internet business.

With everything taken into account, Wix is an extraordinary alternative for basic portfolios and sites run by individuals who don't need an excessive amount of issues.

The drawback is that you'll have less authority over the back-finish of your site and generally speaking execution. You may likewise think that it's trickier to incorporate progressed highlights like shopping baskets and email information exchange structures.

4. Shopify

Geniuses – Simple, speedy online store arrangement.

Cons – Pro highlights are costly.

Cost of set up – 'Essential' bundle begins at $29 every month.

Shopify, as the name recommends, is made particularly for online stores.

The plan and format are basic and clear. Once more, there's no coding required so you can get ready for action in the blink of an eye. Indeed, Ben coordinated it from beginning to end and it required only 19 minutes to make a Shopify store.

The genuine excellence of Shopify is the incorporated online business highlights. It naturally handles installments, dispatching rates, charges, and request following. For an extra charge, you can likewise utilize their implicit advertising support and coordinate the product with a certifiable store to rearrange your records.

The option in contrast to Shopify is utilizing WordPress with a module called WooCommerce. When all is said in done, WordPress and WooCommerce work out less expensive regarding exchanges and level expenses. In any case, you're paying for straightforwardness and convenience.

The disadvantage is that you have less command over the hidden engineering of your site. This is the place where WordPress and Woocommerce are more adaptable, however with that comes extra work and support.

Reward: 7 Ways To Get Seen

Picking the correct stage and setting it up is simply stage one. The following stage is getting seen. Shockingly, there are no alternate ways here, and traffic won't show up consequently. Here at seven deceives you can use to begin driving individuals to your site or social records:

1. Facebook adverts

Cost – I spend generally $100 every week on Facebook advertisements, yet you can positively begin with less. Others will burn through thousands once they can ensure a rate of profitability.

Facebook adverts are probably the most ideal approaches to take advantage of a super-focused on the crowd. You have full oversight over the socioeconomics, area, and interests of your crowd so you just elevate to individuals that are intrigued.

Use adverts to educate individuals concerning your site and how you will tackle their issues. Facebook advertisements are reasonable as well. I prompt testing them out on a limited scale first, at that point expanding the spend continuously.

For more data, look at my manual for expanding active visitor clicking percentage on Facebook adverts.

2. Site design improvement (SEO)

Cost – There's no monetary expense here (except if you recruit a specialist), just the time engaged with exploring and executing the strategies.

Web optimization is tied in with getting your site positioned in Google look. It's a HUGE point that merits a whole book of information to dominate (in spite of the fact that, this asset from the people at Moz is an incredible spot to begin).

Your absolute initial step here is choosing what 'catchphrases' you need to rank for. As such, what should individuals type into Google to discover you? (We have a convenient blog to help you locate the best catchphrases for your business).

Next, do some basic 'on-page' streamlining. Spot those catchphrases 'on the page' in your title labels, headers, picture portrayals, and labels and so forth This is simply basic preparation and establishment working for what's to come.

'Genuine world' organizations like bistros or cafés will likewise need to guarantee their guide area on Google and show themselves on registries on the web. Discover more about 'nearby SEO' here.

3. Begin creating content

Cost – Writing web journals are totally free. Notwithstanding, in the event that you like to enlist a consultant, it will cost between $0.10 – $0.20 per word at sites like Problogger and UpWork.

Sites, recordings, and pictures are the most ideal approach to begin speaking with your crowd and producing some clamor. Content causes you to arrive at possible clients and build up your image.

Consider your present online media newsfeeds. They are loaded with content expected to interface with you and construct a group of people. It requires some investment to compose a blog or produce a video, however, it's certainly justified regardless of the exertion in question.

Regardless of what industry you are in, content encourages you to enhance your guests. It shows your aptitude, helps fabricate a character and draws more traffic. Take a stab at perusing our manual for making a substance technique that drives hard traffic.

4. Start visitor posting

Cost – Again, this is free except if you wish to employ an expert essayist.

Delivering content is a decent beginning, however, how would you get individuals to see it? One path is to deliver content for existing sites and sites. It's an opportunity to get your name before another crowd and associate with those in the business.

Have a go at composing a visitor blog and contributing it to another blog your specialty. In the event that they acknowledge it, you'll get a connection back to your site and your substance will ideally rouse another crowd to follow you. (Connections back to your site are likewise basic for site design improvement).

(Back To Top)

5. Influencer promoting

Cost – It can be free in the event that you approach the correct individuals and offer complimentary advancement. Moving toward the most mainstream influencers anyway can cost from \$50 to \$15,000+ to advance your item.

Influencers are those with tremendous followings and validity in your industry. Influencer advertising is getting increasingly more impressive on the web, with some online media accounts piling up a large number of supporters. By taking advantage of their current crowd, you can cause them to notice you and your business.

Obviously, it is difficult, and at times it costs an expense on the off chance that you'd like the influencer to include your item. Nonetheless, on the off chance that you pick the correct blog or individual, it can drive a great deal of focused traffic to you.

Start by distinguishing key influencers in your industry. Start a discussion with them over Twitter or send them an obliging email. Attempt to assemble a shared relationship before you request something.

6. Convey a public statement

Cost – PR appropriation begins at around $100.

A public statement is an archive that informs the world concerning you. You can draw in an organization to draft and convey a decent public statement for your organization and it shouldn't cost a great deal. Here is an official statement we did when we updated our worker speed checker and we were fortunate to have the news gotten by Yahoo.

Favorable to tip: start by featuring something important about your business. Attempt to adopt the thought process of a writer or blogger and comprehend what might make them need to expound on you. Is there something one of a kind about your item or plan of action? Is it accurate to say that you are dispatching something creative or noteworthy? Incorporate some backstory about yourself and give the blogger a 'story' to create. At that point discover an organization to appropriate it.

(Back To Top)

7. Remember certifiable advertising!

Cost – Word of mouth costs nothing, however in case you're creating limited-time materials the cost will shift contingent upon the amount you make.

In the online world, it's anything but difficult to fail to remember how amazing conventional showcasing can be. Make certain to remember connections to your online presence for your business card and special materials. It's even worth seeking after adverts in exchange magazines and specialty distributions to get the news out.

Ends

There is nobody size-fits-all arrangement with regards to an online presence.

An unpredictable site isn't really the most appropriate response for you, particularly in case you're simply beginning. There are alternate ways and simpler alternatives, for example, a basic online media account or a direct portfolio page.

Try not to put resources into a precarious site on the off chance that you esteem straightforwardness. However, similarly, don't oblige yourself in case you're assembling a veritable computerized business.

To begin with, choose what you need from your online presence. Second, coordinate the stage to your necessities. Third, utilize dynamic advancement to expand on that online presence. To recap, here is the line up for each of the four stages.

10

Start Blogging!

Have you generally needed to begin a blog?

In case you're an essayist, it bodes well: You can utilize a blog to fill in as your writer stage, market your work or find new independent composing customers. Contributing to a blog is likewise an incredible method to try different things with your composing style.

In case you're looking for a decent method to share your considerations, emotions and mastery, presently is an extraordinary chance to begin a blog.

(Furthermore, no, there aren't an excessive number of sites out there as of now!)

This is the period of substance — individuals are continually searching for additional to ingest, and your extraordinary voice has a spot on the immense, boundless interwebs, as well.

We're here to assist you with exploring step so you can begin a blog calm — from picking your space name to distributing your first post.

Here's the way to begin a blog.

1. Pick a space name (and get that area name for nothing)

First of all: setting up a blog. Where are individuals going to discover you on the web? As an author, you are your image, so we suggest utilizing some variety of your name.

To check accessibility, basically, visit Bluehost and snap on "new space." Or, search this convenient area name checker!

Regardless of whether yourname.com isn't accessible, you may discover it with an alternate closure, for example, yourname.co or yourname.io. In case you're overly dedicated to this entire composing thing, you can likewise take a stab at attaching a "author" onto the finish of your name, as in susanshainwriter.com.

Then again, you could choose an inventive blog name — however, recollect your inclinations and target crowd may change as the years pass by. At the point when I began publishing content to a blog in 2012, I zeroed in exclusively on experience travel and named my blog Travel Junkette. Subsequent to extending my specialty and administrations, I changed to susanshain.com on the grounds that my name won't change, regardless of what I'm contributing to a blog about.

Despite the fact that it was certifiably not an immense arrangement, I wish I'd began utilizing my name as space, and would exhort you not to commit a similar error I did.

Whenever you've chosen your area (or areas, in case you're similar to a large number of us writepreneurs!), don't stand by to get it. Regardless of whether you're not prepared to begin a blog at this moment, spaces are modest — and you would prefer not to chance to lose the one you need.

In case you're truly struggling to pick a URL, survey our more itemized present on how on pick a space name.

Before you really click "buy," however, you should peruse the subsequent stage; we will reveal to you how to get an area name for nothing.

2. Buy a facilitating bundle

Presently it's an ideal opportunity to pick a web to have.

What's a web have? Indeed, your facilitating organization does all the specialized sorcery to ensure your site really shows up when individuals type your space name into their program. At the end of the day, it's quite significant.

While we use MediaTemple to have The Write Life, it's normally better for online journals with heaps of traffic, so you likely needn't bother with that in case you're simply beginning.

For another blog, attempt Bluehost. It's utilized by top bloggers around the globe and is known for its client care and dependability.

The Write Life has an association with Bluehost whereby they permit our perusers to buy facilitating for $2.95/month. The cool part is that INCLUDES your area.

Goodness, and master consultant tip: Put your buy (and all the buys recorded in this post) on a business Mastercard and keep the receipts; as interests in your business, they're charge deductible.

3. Introduce WordPress

We're practically through with the geek stuff, we guarantee!

You have a few distinct options for writing for a blog stage, however, we like WordPress best. Not exclusively is it thoroughly free, however, it's anything but difficult to learn, offers a wide assortment of subjects, and has an online network and plenitude of modules that make publishing content to a blog available to everyone.

You can peruse thorough directions for introducing WordPress on your new blog here. Whenever you've finished that, you can formally sign into your blog and begin making it look pretty.

4. Put your site in "support mode"

While dealing with your blog's appearance, you should set up an "underdevelopment" sign to welcome guests.

You don't need any possible customers or perusers to Google your name and locate a half-completed site. (You may believe you will wrap setting up your blog tomorrow, however, we as whole expertise journalists linger when there are no approaching cutoff times!)

To set up upkeep mode, simply download this module. On your upkeep page, you could even incorporate a connection to your email bulletin or online media profiles so guests have a substitute method of connecting with you. At the point when you're prepared to impart your blog to the world, basically deactivate and erase the module.

5. Pick a blog topic

Presently we're getting to the pleasant stuff! Your subject figures out what your blog resembles, and you have a ton of alternatives to browse. Truly, there's a wide scope of free topics, yet in case you're not kidding about contributing to a blog, the customization and backing offered by paid subjects can't be beaten.

Here at The Write Life, we use Genesis, which is perhaps the most mainstream premium subjects accessible. Another famous and adaptable subject is Thesis.

On my first blog, I utilized Elegant Themes, which has a wide determination of wonderful subjects at a sensible cost. These topics accompany limitless help — fundamental when you're beginning a blog.

On the off chance that you need your blog to be a promoting instrument for your composing administrations, you may search for a topic with a static landing page (like mine). That way, your site will look proficient and speaking to everybody — regardless of whether they're there to peruse your most recent post or recruit you for a task.

Whatever you do, ensure your topic is "responsive," which implies it naturally changes with look great on any gadget. Since the greater part of the site, visits are made on cell phones, this is vital for your blog's tasteful.

6. Make a blog header

I believe it's consistently worth getting a custom header for another blog.

You can ask your #1 visual fashioner, make one with Canva or request one on Fiverr. I've had incredible karma getting headers and different illustrations planned in this online commercial center, where a great many individuals offer their administrations for $5 per gig.

Beginning a blog can appear to be a ton of work - yet we've made it simple with this bit by bit manage only for authors. Here's the way to begin a blog without any preparation.

7. Compose your blog pages

In spite of the fact that you're beginning a blog and not a static site, you'll actually need a couple of pages that don't change. ("Pages" are unique in relation to "posts," which are the day by day/week after week/month to month sections you distribute on your blog.)

Here are a few pages you might need to make:

About

The about page is habitually promoted as perhaps the most-saw pages on sites, so don't disregard it. Incorporate an expert headshot and brief bio, and clarify why you're writing for a blog and why the peruser should mind. What makes you a specialist? How might you help them?

Try not to be reluctant to allow your character to radiate through — writing for a blog is an individual issue!

Contact

You need your perusers to have the option to connect with you, correct? At that point, you'll require a contact page.

It doesn't need to be anything extravagant; simply advise your perusers how best to contact you. Try not to put your full email address on here, as spambots could get tightly to it. To workaround that, you can utilize a contact structure module, which we'll connect to beneath, or just compose something like "yourname AT yoursite DOT com."

Portfolio

It's your blog, so parade what you have! Show your imminent customers and perusers that you merit their time and consideration with instances of your over a significant time span of work.

You can see instances of incredible author portfolios here; actually, I love Sara Frandina's.

Assets

Do you have a rundown of most loved composing devices? Or then again perhaps books that have motivated you? Perusers love assets pages, and for bloggers, they can likewise be a sharp method to acquire payment from partner deals. Look at The Write Life's assets page for motivation.

Start here

You presumably won't require this from the outset, yet a "start here" page is brilliant once you have a respectable measure of substance. It's an incredible occasion to communicate your central goal and feature your best work, so your perusers can see the estimation of your blog without swimming through months' or years' worth of posts.

Joanna Penn works admirably with hers, urging perusers to download her digital book and afterward pick a subject that intrigues them.

Work with me

In case you're utilizing your new blog to sell your composing administrations, this page is basic. Be clear about how you can help individuals and how they can connect with you. You could even rundown bundles of various administrations, as Lisa Rowan does on her site.

Whenever you've set up the entirety of your pages, ensure they're effectively open from the landing page. On the off chance that they're not appearing, you may need to change your menus.

8. Introduce modules

Modules are extraordinary for everyone, particularly those of us who are less OK with the specialized side of things. Consider them applications for your blog; they're free devices you can introduce to do an assortment of things.

In spite of the fact that having bunches of modules can sabotage the usefulness and security of your blog, there are a few we suggest everybody investigate:

Better Click-to-Tweet: Encourage perusers to share your substance by including a tick-to-tweet box inside your posts. This module makes it simple.

Contact Form 7: If you need to try not to put your email address on your contact page, utilize this module, which is as often as possible refreshed and gets great surveys.

Hi Bar: Want to get perusers to pursue your free bulletin? Or on the other hand, need to declare the arrival of your most recent book? This module permits you to make a standard for the highest point of your blog.

Mashshare: These offer catches are like the ones you see here on The Write Life. Another moderate alternative is the Simple Share Buttons Adder. It doesn't make a difference which module you pick; it's only essential to make social sharing simple for your perusers.

Google Analytics Dashboard: This module tracks the guests to your site so you can perceive what individuals are keen on and how they're discovering you.

Akismet: One of the migraines of publishing content to a blog is the plenty of spam remarks. This module will assist you in decreasing the number of spammers that sneak through.

WP Super Cache: Another module that is not attractive, but rather is significant. Storing permits your blog to stack quicker — satisfying both your perusers and Google.

Yoast SEO: This across-the-board SEO module encourages you to enhance your posts so you can get natural traffic from web indexes.

9. Introduce gadgets

On the off chance that your blog has a sidebar, you should tidy it up with a couple of gadgets, otherwise known as little boxes with various capacities. All things considered, the moderate look is in — so skirt this progression in the event that you need to keep your sidebar basic.

Here are a few thoughts:

About box

You've likely observed this on a lot of online journals; it's a case in the upper right-hand corner inviting you to the webpage. Look at The Write Life overseeing manager Jessica Lawlor's blog for a genuine model.

Online media symbols

Make it simple for your perusers to follow you via online media by remembering to connect to your profiles for the sidebar. Your subject will presumably incorporate this element, yet on the off chance that not, here's a fundamental instructional exercise.

Well known posts

Whenever you've been contributing to a blog for some time, you should feature your most mainstream posts in the sidebar, which you can do with an essential content gadget. We do this here on The Write Life so you can locate our most famous substance rapidly and without any problem.

10. Buy reinforcement programming

Try not to disregard this significant advance since you don't have content yet! It's smarter to introduce this product right on time than to begin writing for a blog and fail to remember until it's past the point of no return.

Free choices exist, yet I've never had the best of luck with them — and for something as significant as my whole blog, I wouldn't fret paying some extra. (It's a business discount, recall?!) Popular reinforcement alternatives incorporate VaultPress, BackupBuddy, and blogVault.

11. Start your email list

I know, I know — you haven't begun publishing content to a blog, and I as of now need you to fabricate an email list. Trust me; you'll be so happy you did.

Alexis Grant, the author of The Write Life, concurs with me. "On the off chance that I could return and do one thing another way for my business, it would be beginning a bulletin prior," she composes. "My email list is THAT significant for my business, carrying traffic to my site, purchases of my items and openings I never could've anticipated."

Regardless of whether you don't have anything to send, simply begin gathering email addresses. The most ideal approach to allure individuals to join is by offering a free digital book or asset. For an incredible model, look at The Write Life's Freelance Writer Pitch Checklist.

My number one email pamphlet stage is Mailchimp. It's natural, fun, and free for up to 2,000 supporters. There are numerous instruments to browse, however; here are a couple of more alternatives for building your email list.

Whenever you've made your rundown, urge your perusers to join by adding a membership box to your sidebar, and possibly introducing a module like PopupAlly.

12. Compose!

On the off chance that you truly need to begin a blog, you will have to... begin publishing content to a blog.

We suggest making a publication schedule — regardless of whether it's simply you contributing to a blog. It doesn't need to be extravagant; it can even be written out on a notepad.

What's significant is that you plan your posts ahead of time, so you can monitor your thoughts and adhere to a timetable. It's likewise an opportunity to survey and change your substance methodology. What would you like to expound on? In what capacity will you attract perusers?

Remember you're composing for the web, so your style should be unique in relation to the event that you were composing for print. Keep your tone conversational, use "you" expressions to address the peruser, and separate content with list items and sub-headers. Ultimately, remember SEO, and get a component photograph from locales like Unsplash and Pexels to make each post sparkle.

13. Advance, advance, advance

You're nearly there! Since you've begun composing, it's an ideal opportunity to get perusers. What's more, I would rather not be the unfortunate messenger, yet for some authors, this is the most shockingly tedious part of publishing content to a blog. In spite of the fact that it'd be pleasant in the event that we could simply compose (that is the thing that we love to do, right?), it's more pleasant to have individuals really read your work.

You can attempt visitor posting on different online journals, reposting on locales like Medium and LinkedIn, or remembering joins when composing reactions for gatherings, Facebook gatherings, or on Quora. Simply ensure you're adding esteem — and not spamming individuals with your URL.

Web-based media is another extraordinary method to get more traffic and develop your creator following. Rather than only gloating, make certain to interface with editors, authors and bloggers, too. Share their substance with your locale, remark on their posts, and backing them when and where you can. Ideally, they'll give back in kind!

Eventually, making an effective blog is about difficult work and consistency. Continue posting accommodating and drawing in substance, advancing it for SEO, and imparting it to your organizations — and you'll before long observe your new blog begin to bloom.

Congrats, you've presently authoritatively begun a blog as an essayist. Get it's an ideal opportunity to get composing!

11

Follow in the Footsteps of an Expert to become an expert too!

A solid individual brand is basic in the present proficient market, however, it's hard to tell where to begin. Here are straightforward strides on the best way to fabricate a viable brand to turn into a specialist in your field.

What's your opinion about when you hear "Master?" or "Marking"?

For some, experts, firm logos, mottos, site style, and administrations ring a bell. Not to belittle the significance of these variables, but rather these days these are just a little division of the general proficient achievement fixings.

These days, there is no uncertainty that turning into a specialist in your field makes you more significant and clear quicker approaches to prevail in a packed proficient world.

Developing an individual brand and master position frequently needs some external help and aptitude however as consistently there are quick approaches to arrive at it.

Yet, beyond a shadow of a doubt: Whether you concur with our position and if you purposefully make your own band, you DO have an individual brand.

As Jeff Bezos, the organizer of Amazon, once stated: "Your image is the thing that individuals state about you when you are not in the room".

Most experts, in any case, have not dealt with their brands as of not long ago and may not have placed a lot of thought into it.

They are simply may not know about it.

There is a far-reaching conviction that in the event that you put forth a valiant effort at function as an expert somebody will take note.

That was valid previously.

Nowadays, by and large, sadly, that isn't sufficient. Particularly when numerous adjustments in innovation and the economy have influenced it.

It's imperative to be purposeful with regard to your own image. Attempt these five stages to turning into a specialist and you, as well, can begin fabricating yours:

1. From what you never really interest you

As an expert, let me accept, you are as of now a specialist or are en route to getting one, at any rate in the field you are right now working in.

Isn't that so?

Thus, why not beginning in that general area.

Assessing your present position will be your initial step. It will permit you to inspect the likelihood to expand upon your present ability and develop from that point.

In any case, I can hear some of you previously asking: imagine a scenario in which I need to change.

Imagine a scenario where you are not inspired by the thing you are presently doing and need to construct your mastery in different territories.

All things considered, your primary goal is to discover and sort out what truly interests you at the present time.

What is the main piece of this cycle?

It is to discover the "thing" that you decide to be a specialist in, that you are nearly fixated on.

At the end of the day, it needs to move you so the essential perusing and learning appear to be easy to you since you appreciate the learning cycle, it thoroughly impacts you.

Keep in mind: in view of my work with a great many experts – attorneys, bookkeepers, charge guides, and so forth – from everywhere the world, I never met an expert (or even an individual) with no skill. Everybody has one–some have more than one–you simply need to discover it.

2. Build up your particular perspective on one subject

One of the genuine deterrents for some legal counselors in building up their own image is the need to center and build up their 'unmistakable perspective' on just one subject.

Numerous legal counselors accept, erroneously, that on the off chance that they will zero in on one subject they will botch the chances that may come from different regions they can help and support their customers on.

Here is reality – attempting to turn into a specialist in such a large number of things all at once will just set you up for disappointment.

You likely heard before the idiom – in the event that you center around everything, you will get nothing!

Core interest.

The straightforward mystery is: Focus on one subject. Do it well. Over and over. Become a specialist.

3. Practice x 3

Turning into a specialist requires some investment. Critical time.

Be that as it may, numerous experts previously put a great deal of work and commitment into turning into a specialist in their field.

So to frame and keep up your master position, I heartily propose to you to commit some an ideal opportunity for:

Considering—Experts are likewise understudies forever. Keep on understanding books; go to on the web and disconnected schooling exercises or online classes; watch recordings; go to gatherings, occasions, and workshops; share information and gain from different specialists inside the field.

Rehearsing—really actualizing and doing what you are realizing. Expanding your organization of associations in your field and practice things you learned in your examination time.

Introducing—Part of being a specialist is figuring out how to impart your ability and finding to your clan and pertinent individuals. These days, there are numerous approaches to share your insight, by articles, web journals, eBooks, recordings, webcasts, talking at a gathering, composing a book, and so on

Attempt to discover the channels that work for you and use them to share your ability. Sharing your insight and what you have figured out how to others will push you considerably further toward your objective of dominating your new field and turning into the master.

IT IS YOUR TIME!

Your own image is the entirety of what you do, how you do it, and why you do it.

Your own image must be certified and legitimate. You can't phony it!

On the off chance that you take care of business, your own image will make you as an expert hang out in the jam-packed commercial center, focus on your ability, and improve your worth.

What's more, the potential gain is that in the event that you have genuinely discovered your blessing your thing—your particular perspective – than turning into a specialist in your field should be a euphoric and energizing cycle for you.

On the off chance that this isn't the situation...

... you have settled on some unacceptable decision and you need to return from the earliest starting point.

In this stage there are as yet numerous inquiries left unanswered – Isn't there a demonstrated way to building your position?

A particular instrument that can help construct your power?

How might you utilize your position to pull in additional from the correct customers to your firm? And so on

These and more in the following piece of this exceptional arrangement.

12

How Seth Godin Built his personal brand?

Seth Godin is maybe perhaps the most broadly read advertisers on the planet, and all things considered. His long line of successes has been pushing the envelope in advertising for quite a long time.

Today we'll remove some vital exercises from his hit "The Bootstrapper's Bible," and apply them to your own marking endeavors. In the most straight-forward terms, bootstrapping implies doing a great deal with a bit. It's the way of thinking I've utilized from the very beginning with my business: getting the most value for your money, particularly when you begin with basically nothing. How about we perceive how Godin's bootstrapping tips can cause the time you to spend on close to home marking pack all the more a punch.

Bootstrapping tips

1. Quit arranging and begin doing. Get out there and do it. The more you do, the more you do. Entryways will open. Openings will show up. Your model will change, your standing will build, you will end up being a magnet for savvy individuals. Yet, none of this will occur on the off chance that you remain inside and continue arranging. Pick something on your rundown and get it done.

2. Position yourself against the brand chief. Be shameless in the manner you contrast yourself with an innovator in your field. Your story should be short, strong, and noteworthy. Would you be able to be "less expensive than Frito's" or "quicker then Federal Express?" in your particular specialty? The more your adversary gets advanced, the more your situating explanation increments in worth.

3. Be shockingly tireless. It's not about what you know or even what you do. Achievement is about determination. Set sensible assumptions and don't surrender. Never take no for an answer except for being deferentially constant.

4. Partner with champs. Four gatherings of individuals will significantly impact how your business advances:

- Clients
- Workers
- Sellers
- Companions

5. Offer courtesies to free. The most ideal approach to discover peers is to commit a few hours seven days offering courtesies to individuals. Favors with no aim of being reimbursed. Offer a few courtesies to outsiders and some for companions:

Send somebody an important news cut-out or email message

Allude business to another organization that can deal with it better than you

This is the means by which you assemble trust and generosity among the individuals who can help get you where you need.

6. Be a connector to build up a solid friend gathering. Interface with individuals by associating them to one another. A couple of hours seven days will net you a gathering of at least 100 companions who will profit by your endeavors as much as you'll profit by theirs.

Look at your neighborhood office of trade, nearby CEO club, or start one yourself.

Do the accompanying to fortify your gathering:

Discover occasions to gloat about and praise different organizations and individuals you know

On the off chance that you talk with somebody who's fabulous however not for you, send that individual to a companion (you just made two companions!)

In the event that you compose an article and need a contextual investigation, request that a friend contribute

On the off chance that you manage a business and you're content with the experience, compose a letter to the president and, organizer to the originator, let her expertise she did.

Make certain to go along with one that is as playful and empowering as you seem to be. You need to encircle yourself with individuals who have succeeded are as yet appreciating the ride.

7. Accomplice and work with bigger brands (individuals or organizations). Make a commonly useful relationship with greater, more extravagant, more steady associations. You can bring in cash quicker, open admittance to assets, and produce believability.

Some large organization authors scorn what their organization has become.

They rail against the gradualness, organization, and failure to complete anything any longer. What they need is somebody like you who can take on a particular assignment and transform organization resources into gold. You'll be astounded at how effectively you can permit a brand name or do bargains for promotion space or assume control over ventures for a major organization. Now and then they'll settle in advance, just to amplify the opportunity of progress.

With these seven hints, you're well headed to getting the most value for your money with your own image. What time-powerful close to home marking strategies do you utilize that epitomize Godin's bootstrapper outlook?

13

How Neil Patel built his personal brand?

Today we will discuss individual marking, which I believe is progressively significant. There are a ton of influencers, individuals on Snapchat, individuals on Instagram, on YouTube, who are turning out to be branded with tremendous followings. Obviously, a ton of advertisers is beginning to work with influencers to an ever-increasing extent.

In any case, how might you become an influencer and influence your own image by the day's end?

Turning into a Household Name in Marketing

Neil is an extraordinary contextual investigation—the Neil Patel brand is gigantic and almost an "easily recognized name" with regards to web-based promoting. That is on the grounds that Neil is extremely centered around building his image and indeed has made a big deal about an everyday occupation out of it.

For what reason does Neil invest more energy on close to home marking than on marking his sites (despite the fact that he does that a ton, as well)? How about we do a basic psychological study: Do you associate more with Coca Cola, or Lebron James, or Kim Kardashian? Odds are, you associate more with a person than with a corporate brand.

That is the reason I accept individual marking is one of the most grounded and most significant things you could be investing your time, energy, and cash in as an advertiser.

Take a gander at Gary Vaynerchuk, who runs VaynerMedia. He has extraordinary compared to other known individual brands of a business visionary. He's dynamic on Snapchat and YouTube and his webcast is all over. Like the universe, his image is consistently growing. In the event that you go to Google Trends, which is an extraordinary device for taking a gander at how large these brands truly are, you can see his trendline over the long run:

The hardest thing is building a crowd of people. It requires some investment. Many individuals currently are stating, "Indeed, it may bode well to fabricate that crowd first before you even attempt to sell anything."

Begin Building Your Personal Brand with Social Media

In the event that you need to begin with close to home marking, start with your social profiles. At the point when you get a companion demand on Facebook, for instance, regardless of whether you don't have any acquaintance with them, add them. Why? Since when you share something, an individual picture, something about your business, something about your leisure activities, or whatever it very well might be—that is one more individual who will be seeing you. What's more, that one individual has a huge organization.

Start off with Facebook, Twitter, Instagram, and Snapchat. Influence these famous online media locales, share your "typical day for," share what you're doing to realize, or your corporate stuff, or your business stuff, whatever it could be, and develop from that point.

Add every one of your companions that you definitely know, at that point cross-advance your social profiles with one another. For instance, in case you're on Twitter, advise individuals to follow you on Facebook. On Facebook, advise individuals to follow you on Twitter. For Instagram, advise individuals to follow you on Snapchat and the other way around.

Pair up Snapchat and Instagram together, on the grounds that they have a comparative kind of crowd. What's more, pair up Twitter and Facebook together, as well. At the point when you cross-advance that way, you get an ever-increasing number of fans.

There are likewise Twitter devices you can use to naturally follow individuals inside your space or the space you need to be marked in. Furthermore, when they follow you back, that is a simple win. On the off chance that they don't follow you back, following half a month, it eliminates them. Thusly, you can develop your Twitter by continuing in a natural way.

Marking Requires a great deal of Patience

At the point when I originally began doing my Growth Everywhere web recording, I didn't have a goal. It was truly a show proactive kindness leisure activity. No one on my radar was convincing to business visionaries and truly plunging to showcase strategies that work, or what assisted them with getting their initial 100 or 1,000 clients.

Presently we're coming to around 70,000 individuals every month. It's just been around more than two years, and it will get greater and greater, as long as I remain steady with it.

The key is to give a ton of significant worth to your crowd. It's not simply, "Goodness I'm going to post photos of my food, or this is me celebrating." You need to sort out what kind of significant worth you can give to your crowd. This is the means by which you fabricate you're continuing in a supportable way.

Neil requested one from his pals, "Hello, out of the multitude of things you've done, what has assisted you with developing your image more than everything else?" He has a famous blog, he does YouTube recordings, he does interviews, he's been on TV, he's composed a book. His mate really advised him, "Neil, the main thing that is developed my image more than all else was composing a book." That's the reason Neil composed Hustle.

The other thing Neil does to develop his image reliably blogs. Blogging on his own site, however, visitor posting on locales like Entrepreneur, Forbes, Inc., and so on The first occasion when he hit up Forbes, they had no clue about what his identity was, despite the fact that he was at that point genuinely known in the showcasing scene at that point. So don't be debilitating—simply be tenacious with editors.

The most effortless approach to get an in with one of the editors is to coordinate with the absolute visitor donors there. These are individuals, like Neil, who compose on Forbes for nothing, for entertainment only and to extend their image mindfulness.

A chilly effort message Neil has a ton of progress with resembles this:

"Hello, Jason, large fanatic of yours. I love perusing your articles on Forbes. I saw you composed this article on SEO, yet you didn't make reference to A, B, and C strategy. On the off chance that you did, I figure it would truly help your perusers or your guests, and so forth Cheers, Neil."

What's more, that is it.

Typically Jason will email Neil back and state, "Hello Neil, a debt of gratitude is in order for the criticism. This was incredible." Note that Neil isn't requesting anything, he's simply developing a relationship.

Following a couple of days, Neil may catch up with:

"Hello Jason, love this post that you composed on publishing content to a blog. I cherished it so much that I even shared it on my #1 social locales, Facebook, and Twitter. Appreciate, Neil." That's it. He's generally going to react with, "Much appreciated."

Possibly seven days after the fact, Neil will catch up with him once more. He'll state:

"Hello Jason, I have a fast inquiry for you. I truly love what you're doing and I need to emulate your example. One of my life objectives is to compose for destinations like Forbes, Inc., Entrepreneur. How could you approach composing on Forbes? I can compose astounding substance for Forbes perusers. I don't have the foggiest idea whether will be comparable to yours, yet I couldn't want anything more than to make an effort. Anyway, you can acquaint me with the editorial manager there? Cheers, Neil."

This is entirely Neil landed many position openings, similar to when somebody offered him a $2 million base and commissions of $4 million extra. The person stated, "I was Googling for stuff identified with content advertising and I saw your articles everywhere on the web."

Why? Since he was perusing locales like Inc., Entrepreneur, and Forbes. Visitor posting is immense for brand mindfulness and perceivability.

Some of you may be reasoning, "However Neil's a major brand. He can compose for every one of these locales, no issue. He can compose a book, he can do so much insane stuff." Here's the thing, Neil wasn't generally that large. He needed to begin someplace, as well.

Regardless of whether you start by contributing to a blog, it will develop after some time. You're not going to get results quickly in light of the fact that writing for a blog is presumably a 12-multi month venture before you get any outcomes. The key, as usual, is to be patient and learn deferred satisfaction.

Step Up Your Personal Brand

Several years back, I was welcome to talk at a neighborhood tech occasion in Santa Monica, and there were 50 individuals. I had never done any open talking at all and I was apprehensive as heck, yet you need to begin someplace. You will suck, and that is alright, however ultimately you will begin getting welcomed to more things, you will get more open doors coming in your direction.

Neil consistently discusses the significance of connections, as well. At the point when you're ready to offer gigantic worth, individuals will connect with you. I did an online course as of late, just to my own email list. After the online class, an organization in Brazil contacted me and stated, "Hello, why not come address our crowd. We're doing a meeting with 2,500 individuals in Brazil." So, off I went to Brazil.

Stuff like that will, fortunately, begin to occur, as long as you keep the wheels beating. However, recollect, it requires some serious energy on the off chance that you need individuals to know you as someone who adds an incentive as long as possible.

As Neil likes to state, it requires a very long time to develop a brand, however, it just requires a couple of moments to demolish it. So recall:

Be truly cautious with what you do and how you brand yourself

Work at it, and work at it reliably

Partner with individuals who as of now have solid individual brands

Partner with Bigger Brands than Yourself

For instance, Kim Kardashian is popular. Furthermore, anybody around her will in the long run likewise become celebrated. Neil did likewise in the tech space. He saw some time ago, bloggers like Peter Cashmore from Mashable, Michael Arrington from TechCrunch, or Brian O'Malley from Gigaom were directing colossal crowds.

So Neil hit them all up and stated, "Guess what? I need to help you all with your SEO and your showcasing, and I can get you more traffic. Also, guess what? I'll do everything for nothing. I don't need a solitary dollar." And they were all similar to, "Truly?"

Neil is generally partial to his arrangement with Michael Arrington, organizer of TechCrunch. Neil got Michael over 30% more traffic (which, as you presumably definitely know, it's probably the greatest tribute).

Michael Arrington tribute

When Neil got Michael that traffic, Michael not just elevated him by connecting to him in the sidebar of TechCrunch, he likewise did an email impact to a great deal of his VC companions and financial speculators who put resources into organizations. He advised them, "Hello, you ought to have your portfolio organizations enlist Neil. Look what he never really traffic. He can do this to your portfolio organizations."

Consider when you were back in evaluation school, center school, secondary school, and so on There was consistently a cool child's table in the break room, isn't that so? That is the place where the vast majority of the traffic streams.

So on the off chance that you need to be seen at that table and appreciate that kind of traffic and have others who are truly famous in your space express magnificent things about you, you need to develop your own image and not be reluctant to connect with the rockstars of your industry.

14

How did Gary Vaynerchuk build his personal brand?

For quite a long time, I've been discussing how significant individual marking is.

Yet, we should not get befuddled by the semantics:

Your own image is your standing. Furthermore, your standing in unendingness is the establishment of your vocation.

Individuals don't get this. Playing the long game and building your standing consistently plays out.

In any case, the issue is, individuals see others excelling in the present moment to the detriment of their drawn-out close to the home brand. Thus, they get deceived.

Rather than showing restraint, they go for fast deals. They continue attempting to change over clients on the main cooperation. They attempt to extricate cash, rather than making an encounter.

The brand is about how somebody feels at the time when they connect with you or your business.

All of you have feelings you feel in response to names like "Coca-cola", "IBM", or "McDonald's." Whether positive or negative, you have a response. At the point when you hear my name, you likely get an inclination as well (which I trust is positive).

For instance, in the event that you needed to articulate — I trust you'd state "Gary Vaynerchuk, the person who gave more than asked", or something like that. I need you to consider me somebody who gave huge measures of significant worth.

The best organizations on the planet don't sell. They brand. For instance, Apple never attempts to "convert" you into purchasing an iPhone. Rather they portray the "iPhone experience." They center around marking.

I do likewise.

Not saying you ought to never sell. In any case, individual marking is a lopsidedly important factor that a great many people simply don't zero in on.

In this article, I've assembled a mashup of techniques, tips, and exhortation on building an individual brand I've discussed throughout the long term.

Expectation you get a ton of significant worth from it

1. Great INTENT WINS IN A TRANSPARENT WORLD

In a world with all these informal organizations, everything is straightforward. All that you do is caught — with YouTube, Facebook, Instagram, Snapchat, Twitter, and so on All aspects of your development are on record. Anything you do will be known.

You can't have "various characters" any longer for business, family, and all the other things.

You are who you are currently, in this world.

I discussed this initiative in 2008, and it's considerably more evident today.

In a climate like this, individuals who have a great goal will win. Furthermore, individuals who come from an awful spot will lose.

The web will uncover us all, so take some time to consider what your goals are.

2. HAVE A MEDIA COMPANY MENTALITY

There is no motivation to do something besides act as a media organization in the present computerized age.

Individuals haven't completely gotten a handle on the "consideration move" we're surviving.

Why?

In the course of recent years, we've seen organizations "sell" to us continually. There wasn't "without much substance."

Also, it bodes well. They simply didn't have the sort of chances we have. It was costly to make a business. It was costly to set up a bulletin. It was costly to run advertisements on the radio. It actually is.

In any case, presently, you can deliver as much substance as you need across social stages.

This has prepared for another kind of advertising. Rather than selling continually like organizations used to, you can make supportive, instructive, engaging substance and use it to get deals long haul.

Furthermore, the astounding thing is, the substance you make doesn't need to be identified with what you're selling.

For instance... In this meeting I did with Keith Ferrazzi, a group of people part approached me how to make content for a lawful business:

The appropriate response I gave her was a touch maverick.

I pitched her on beginning a site about golf. Absolutely inconsequential to lawful administrations.

Yet, I realized it'd change her business if, state, in each seventh post, she advanced her real business while utilizing golf as the "habit-forming substance" to pull in a group of people.

3. HACK CULTURE AND BUY ADS TO DISTRIBUTE CONTENT

At the point when individuals get some information about my errors and second thoughts, I battle to concoct smart responses. It isn't so much that I don't commit errors, I'm only unequipped for recalling and harping on them.

Yet, there is one thing I lament:

Not spending enough cash on Google AdWords.

I assembled my father's alcohol business from three to $60 million on the rear of Google AdWords. I purchased catchphrases like "wine" for pennies on the dollar when they were undervalued.

Be that as it may, in the event that I spent more, I would've developed it to many millions.

At this moment, Facebook and Instagram are the undervalued stages. Also, it's astonishing to me the number of individuals isn't making the most of the chance.

Figure out how to advance your substance through advertisements. In the event that you don't have any cash to contribute, flip something on eBay, take that cash, and run advertisements with it.

The subsequent method to stand out enough to be noticed is hacking society.

On the off chance that you can comprehend what's really important in culture, you can make an inconceivable open door for yourself. Culture hacking merits its own blog entry, however, the best exhortation I can give here is to exploit influencers.

Message any individual who has 500–1000+ devotees. Perceive how you can add esteem. Hit them up on Instagram DM.

On the off chance that you have a café, you can offer them a customized coupon with the expectation of complimentary food. In the event that you have a pipes administration, give them a free assessment.

Message them, associate, add esteem, and consequently, they may give some attention to your image.

4. Hear WHAT YOU'RE Saying

Being an individual brand for being an individual brand is normally the snappiest method to not be an individual brand.

The initial step to building a brand is to act naturally mindful about what you need to add to the discussion. You need to comprehend what you do and the things you need to discuss,.

I've jabbered for as long as a decade. Yet, inside an exceptionally restricted territory.

I haven't discussed medical care or international issues. I haven't added my input to each mainstream society circumstance.

I talk about the things I know — correspondence in an advanced world.

In case you're not a specialist yet, you can discuss your cycle of turning into a specialist. Archive the excursion.

5. Report OVER CREATE

On the off chance that you need to be heard via web-based media, you need to put out a LOT of substance.

You should do a long structure video blog or webcast at any rate once every week. You should post on Instagram and Snapchat in any event 6-7 times each day.

Presently, that seems as though a great deal. Furthermore, it is.

However, here's one extraordinary suggestion that will help: Document. Try not to make.

Consider it like Keeping up with the Kardashians versus Star Wars and Friends. One is more useful to make, while different takes some inventiveness in thinking of stories. The first is straightforward for the vast majority (counting myself). The second is harder.

You can experience the way toward creating your life on the web to cause yourself to appear like a "specialist." Or you could simply act naturally.

Probably the greatest misstep that individuals make when fabricating their own image is attempting to "oversell" themselves. They front. They attempt to act greater than they really are.

Actually, it's significantly more important to discuss the cycle than the guidance you figure you should be giving them.

Eventually, the game is basic, my companions. Hear what you're saying, put out substance around it, and run advertisements.

Watch what befalls your own image/business.

6. SHOW DIFFERENT SIDES OF YOUR PERSONALITY

The explanation so numerous influencers get commoditized is on the grounds that they just show one side of their character.

For instance, in case you're an appealing wellness model on Instagram, brands that are hoping to support you will place you in the equivalent "container" as the wide range of various alluring wellness models on Instagram.

A great deal of influencers is frightened to post various sides of their character in light of the fact that those posts won't get as much commitment. In the event that their devotees are following them for a certain something (for example wellness), they won't generally like it when they post about something like food, travel, or business.

However, it's something that will change the course of your own image.

Regardless of whether that is no joke "influencer" hoping to get brand sponsorship, indicating various parts of your character will get individuals more put resources into your excursion. It shows your crowd what your identity is. Regardless of whether various individuals quit following you or quit connecting with you, 30% of your crowd will begin admiring you in an alternate manner.

That is the way to situating your image such that isolates you from every other person in your space.

7. Organize YOUR BRAND OVER SALES

My whole organization is a "botch" on paper. The whole VaynerX machine — PureWow, One37pm, every last bit of it — isn't savvy for me to do. It doesn't help my transient funds.

As a business visionary, I'm in the prime of my profession at this moment. I'm in my 40s. I endeavored to set an incredible establishment for myself in my 20s by building my father's alcohol store to a $60 million income business, and I developed VaynerMedia to $150 million+ in income in a brief timeframe moreover.

It's taken a colossal measure of control for me to spend my late 30s and mid-40s constructing a "structure" for the remainder of my life, particularly since we've had an extraordinary economy for the most recent decade.

It would've been a great deal "more intelligent" for me to adapt my data, sell courses, start brains, and be more forceful with adapting my crowd.

In any case, I realize that organizing my image over transient deals is something that will bring me more regard, adoration, and abundance in the long haul.

It's what I urge every one of you to do. While you're running Facebook advertisements to change over deals, you need to similarly invest energy on marking exercises that bring you zero ROI temporarily — things like doing digital broadcast interviews on others' shows, facilitating occasions, and the sky is the limit from there.

8. BE YOUR 100% AUTHENTIC, TRUE SELF. Try not to "WATER IT DOWN" IN ANY SHAPE OR FORM.

In my 20s, I grew a YouTube show around my family's alcohol business called Wine Library TV.

On that show, I conversed with individuals about wine. I would portray wines in manners that no one else did at that point. I said certain wines possessed a flavor like Whatchamacallit bars, or that a specific wine had an aftertaste like somebody opened a racquetball case.

None of the wine "thought pioneers" at the time had depicted wine thusly.

Portraying wines the manner in which I did bring down the measure of "reach" I had with Wine Library TV. It wasn't something that the Food Network or other TV shows were open to initially.

I actually leave cash on the table right up 'til the present time since I care about genuineness over transient dollars. The way that I revile such a huge amount in so a considerable lot of my recordings restricts the quantity of talking gigs I can get. Yet, I'm from New Jersey, reviling is simply important for how I talk — so I won't dilute it.

Truly, individuals who are "phony" will never last. It resembles hip bounce craftsmen who burn out subsequent to having a couple of successes. It resembles business people who call themselves CEOs and look like it yet doesn't really have the foggiest idea how to maintain a business.

The best system for building an individual brand is to be 100% "you", without watering down your character in any capacity.

9. BE SMART ABOUT HOW YOU DISTRIBUTE YOUR BRAND'S CONTENT

I put out an enormous 86-page deck discussing how I make an appropriate substance around my own image.

There are a ton of moving parts, in any case, this is the centerpiece:

"Column content" alludes to the long-structure sound or video show that you use to infer any remaining substance. It very well may be a video blog, a discussion, a webcast meet, or some other long-structure piece that you can transform into more sound/video/composed substance.

For my image, the column content shows are:

1) DailyVee (my video blog)

2) AskGaryVee (my business Q&A show)

3) PodSessions (a gathering digital recording show where I converse with numerous visitors)

4) Influencer (gatherings I take with rappers, Instagram influencers, business people, and that's just the beginning)

5) Keynotes, meetings, and fireside visits.

I'm a major aficionado of "recording" your life over "making" new substance. The main motivation behind why such countless individuals battle in building their own image is that they don't have time. They don't have the opportunity to plunk down and compose, record a digital broadcast, or get ready and film a video.

Be that as it may, on the off chance that you simply archive your contemplations or your excursion, you don't need to invest a huge load of energy on your substance. What's more, since "quality" is emotional, huge numbers of you would in any case get individuals keen on what you need to state.

When you set up your column content, you can take bits of that substance to repurpose it. You can take a video clasp and cleave it up into "miniature clasps" for Instagram. You could take amazing statements from that cut and make pictures. You could interpret the sound or video and distribute it as a blog entry.

For instance, I did a video meeting in 2018 on Travis Mills' show.

From that video talk, I put out a "miniature" on Instagram from a clasp I was especially energetic about.

I would likewise take noteworthy statements and transform them into pictures, and my essayist would take clasps of things I said and use them in articles.

Yet, don't get it bent: this isn't something you need an enormous group to do. A long time before I ever employed a videographer, I was shooting myself and making content around my own image — regardless of whether it was through Wine Library TV or simply handheld selfie recordings.

There's an unimaginable open door right presently to assemble your image utilizing online media, and it will disappear.

I trust you exploit it

15

Top Tool for boosting your Personal Brand!

1. WiseStamp

Stand apart from the group while sending an email. Make a smooth proficient email signature with all your significant subtleties in minutes.

URL: *https://webapp.wisestamp.com/*

2. HubSpot Email Signature Generator

Another free email signature elective.

URL: *https://www.hubspot.com/email-signature-generator*

Free Branded Link Shortener Tool

3. Rebrandly

Abbreviate connections and brand them with your own area.

URL: *https://www.rebrandly.com/*

Free Video Meme App

4. InShot

Make those in vogue Facebook recordings with text on top and base.

Utilize this free application to make Social Media recordings that get consideration.

URL: *https://apps.apple.com/us/app/inshot-video-editor-music-cut/id997362197*

Free Brand Identity Tools

5. Namech_k

Search a name and discover its accessibility across all the web-based media channels.

URL: *https://namechk.com/*

6. about.me

Make a free single page site posting all your expert subtleties in a la mode way.

URL: *https://about.me/*

Free Branding and Logo Creator

7. Signature Maker

A SaaS instrument that reproduces your transcribed business signature.

URL: *https://signature-maker.net/*

8. Trendy person Logo Generator

Produce cool and hip looking logos for nothing.

URL: *https://www.hipsterlogogenerator.com/*

9. Squarespace Logo

Get logos for nothing yet in low goal with this apparatus.

URL: *https://logo.squarespace.com/*

10. Logaster

A SaaS which makes proficient online logos.

URL: *https://www.logaster.com/*

11. Logo Crisp

Make your logo in only 3 straightforward advances. Browse 10,000 free logo pre-caused plans and afterward to tweak.

URL: *https://www.logocrisp.com/*

12. LogoMakr

A free logo making an instrument with 100% adaptable choices.

URL: *https://logomakr.com/*

Free Reputation Monitoring Tools

13. Brand Yourself

Get a fast standing report about your own image in 60 seconds.

URL: *https://brandyourself.com/*

14. Google Alerts

Set cautions about catchphrases identified with your own image and check who is talking what might be said about you.

URL: *https://www.google.com/alerts*

Free Speaking Engagement Tools

15. SpeakerHub

Make a free speaker profile with the goal that occasion coordinators can discover and recruit you to talk on their next occasion. You can likewise install your speaker profile card on your site.

URL: *https://speakerhub.com/*

16

Conclusion

Regardless of whether you've assembled a compelling individual brand as of now, or in case you're simply beginning, you can grow constantly.

Focusing on the folks at the highest point of their game is an incredible spot to begin. These are individuals who offers extraordinarily attempted and tried exhortation.

Regardless of whether you've heard some of it previously, it's a smart thought to continue reviving yourself, and look after core interest.

- As a Personal Brand, ask yourself a portion of these inquiries:
- It is safe to say that you are sure about what you need to be known for?
- Is it true that you are as a rule genuine?
- It is safe to say that you are being social in the correct spots?
- Is it true that you are truly increasing the value of your crowd's lives?
- Is it true that you are interfacing actually with them in any of your channels?
- Is it accurate to say that you are keeping educated on the thing they are stating about you on the web?

What are some different inquiries you figure individual brands should ask themselves?

Individual marking doesn't need to be everyday work. Here are 7 devices that make it simple to screen and improve your online image.

1. Google Alerts.

You can't bear to pass up discussions about your image.

It's ideal to know when you get a whoop, and proactive checking could mean the distinction between successfully dealing with an emergency and totally failing.

The reality is you should be the first to realize when you're referenced on the web.

Specialty a Google ready alarm to keep steady over your notices or those of your opposition. Choose how frequently you need to get the updates and the rest will deal with itself.

2. Canva

Canva makes computerized planning a snap. Need to fabricate a custom Twitter header or a great slideshow? Possibly a bespoke Pinterest pin or a lovely Infographic?

The sky's the cutoff with Canva and you needn't bother with any plan aptitudes. With so numerous great layouts, you can plan visual components and shadings without worrying over the nature of the outcome.

When you're content with a format, you can utilize it over and over to convey visual substance that your crowd can generally expect and appreciate.

Canva is free with the occasion to get a few formats and highlights for $1 each. I've put in a couple of dollars to a great extent yet you can create astonishing plans without spending a penny.

3. BrandYourself.

In case you're hoping to improve your odds of getting employed or getting drives, at that point, you'll need to watch out for your online presence. Also, BrandYourself's DIY instrument is the one you'll require.

With BrandYourself's instrument, you can follow the development of your indexed lists over the long run. You'll be told when things change, get tips on the best way to improve your online properties to be SEO-accommodating, and realize what to do to help things ascend in list items over the long haul.

The free DIY instrument allows you to follow three online profiles while the $99 every year membership gives you the limitless capacity to follow and improve your indexed lists.

In case you will go through any cash improving your online image, BrandYourself's DIY instrument is the best approach.

4. LinkedIn and Twitter Notifications

LinkedIn and Twitter are ground-breaking networks with tremendous occasions to develop your natural crowd and get more eyeballs on your substance.

Try not to neglect those open doors through the breaks. Require a couple of moments every day to monitor your warnings.

Shortly, you can rapidly react to questions, thank individuals for sharing your substance, and follow up on likely leads.

Put forth an extraordinary attempt to draw in with individuals who like your substance. On the off chance that they set aside the effort to peruse or remark on your article, you owe them a reaction. Furthermore, who knows - an honest discussion today could prompt more business tomorrow.

5. Track Twitter makes reference to.

Remaining current with your notices is acceptable, yet reliably following your Twitter specifies takes it to the following level. With this sort of information, you can return to your rundown whenever to see who makes reference to you the most and cooperate with the clients that merit your consideration.

I like to monitor this data utilizing IFTTT, network access that allows you to computerize activities identifying with your online properties.

The administration works like an information/yield machine. In the event that X occurs, at that point do Y.

I made my own IFTTT formula (don't hesitate to utilize it!) that adds a column to a Google Spreadsheet each time I'm referenced on Twitter.

Use it to discover the individuals who reliably notice you so you can collaborate with them now and again. You'll be pouring fuel on a previously popping fire.

6. Remark alarms.

In the event that you distribute blog content on your site, at that point, you should monitor your remarks.

Individuals may be asking you subsequent inquiries or giving you incredible criticism, however, you'd be sure whether you don't get notices.

An analyst who gets a reaction is substantially more prone to cooperate with your substance again later on. It bodes well, isn't that so? Getting overlooked sucks and getting a reaction feels incredible.

It's extraordinarily simple to get remark alarms. On the off chance that you're utilizing Squarespace, at that point, you'll naturally get warnings about new remarks through email.

In case you're utilizing WordPress, go into Settings — > Discussion, and verify "Email me at whatever point anybody posts a remark."

7. Google Analytics.

Have a site? At that point feel free to introduce Google investigation at this moment. With only a couple of clicks, you can follow the main development measurements and contrast them with earlier months. Discover the number of individuals who are seeing your substance, and figure out which pages are the most mainstream.

See what social profiles allude the most traffic, discover where on the planet your clients come from and realize what pages are making individuals bob.

The measure of understanding is amazing. The test is to take that information, sort out the key takeaways, and decide how you can improve the client experience.